A Walk In The Jungle

By: K.K Ray

Coming December 2016, a new Christmas and Winter Coloring Book.

For the latest updates, and to see my latest art follow me on Twitter: KKRayArt

This book belongs to:

_____

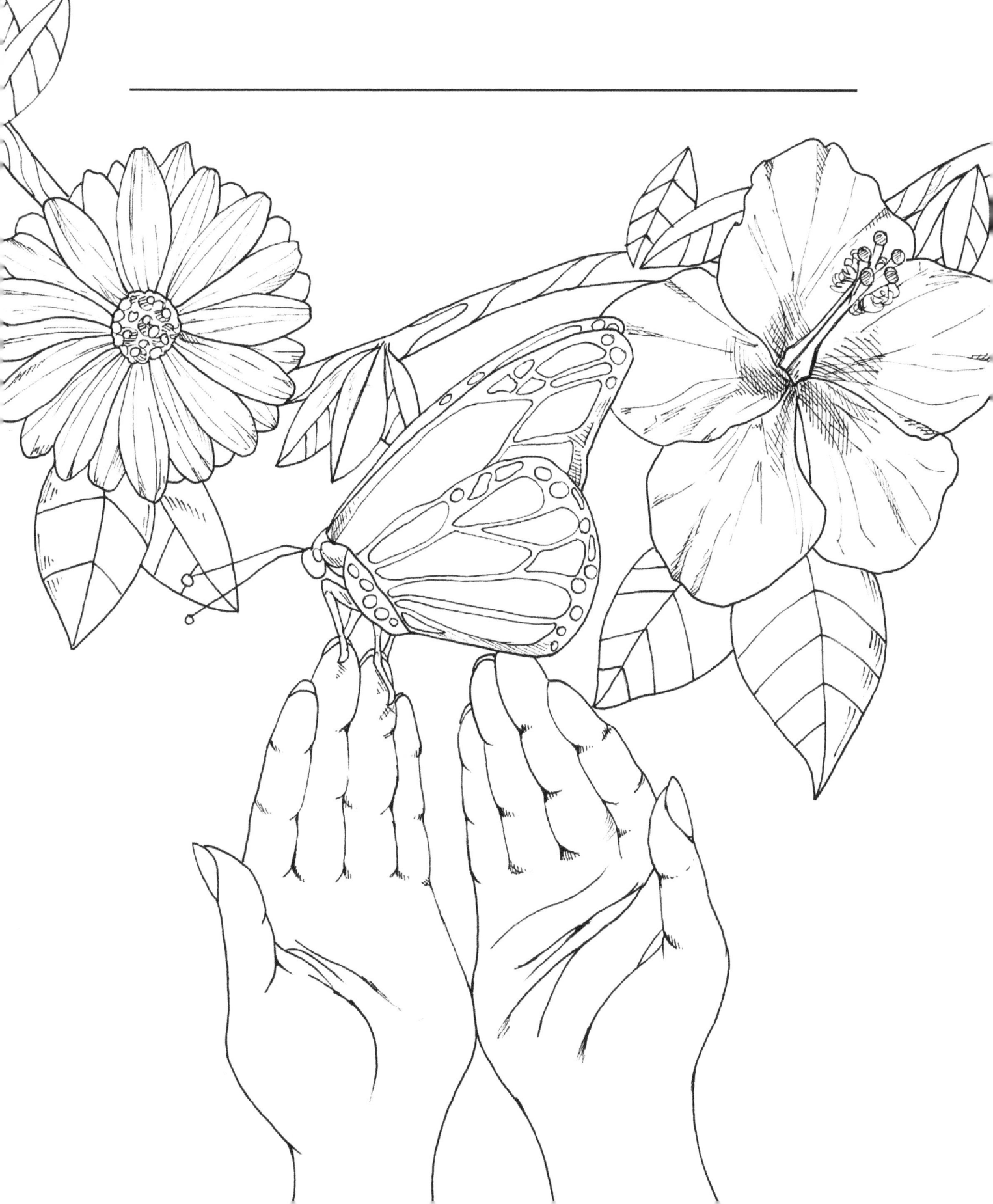

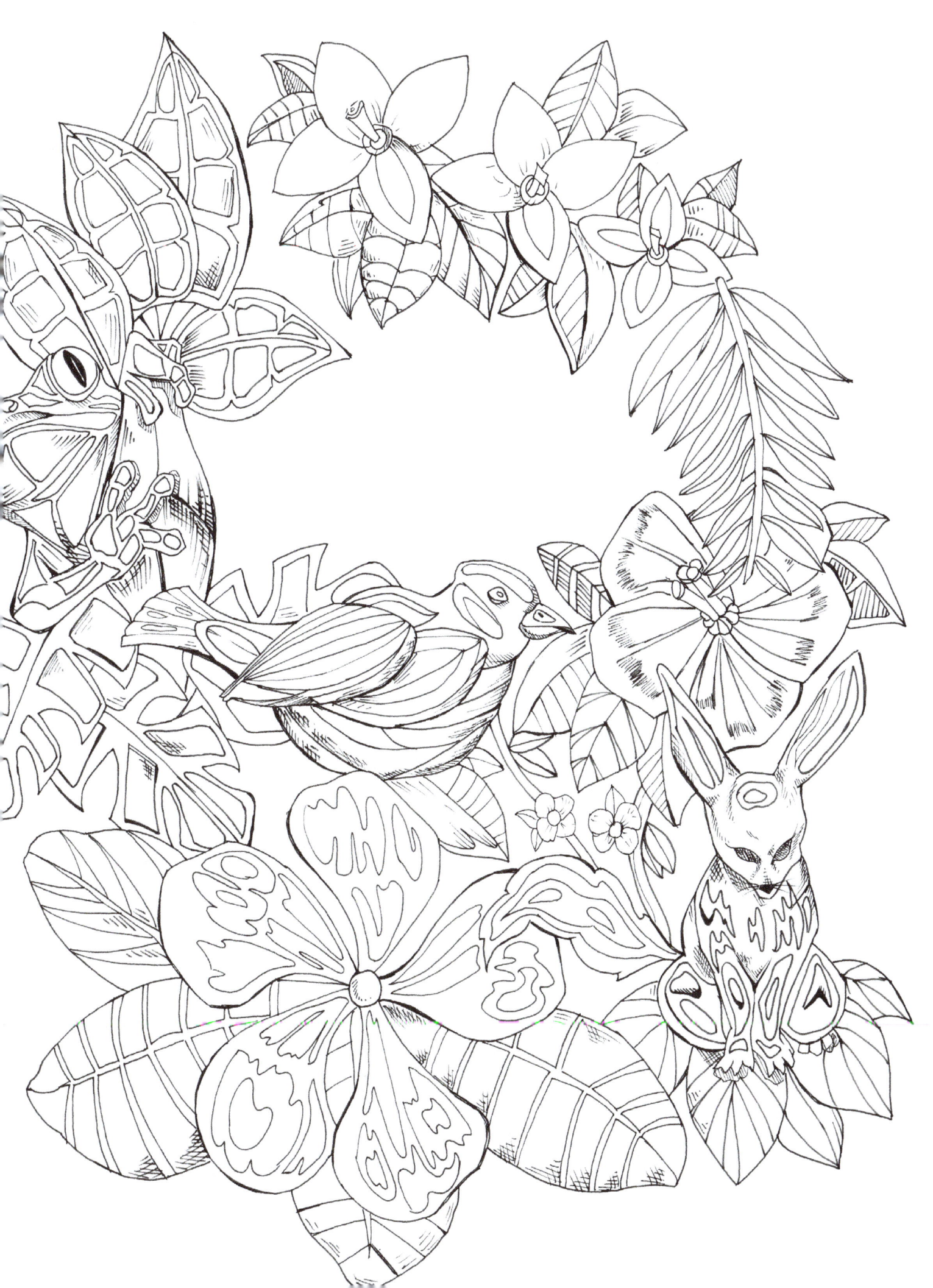

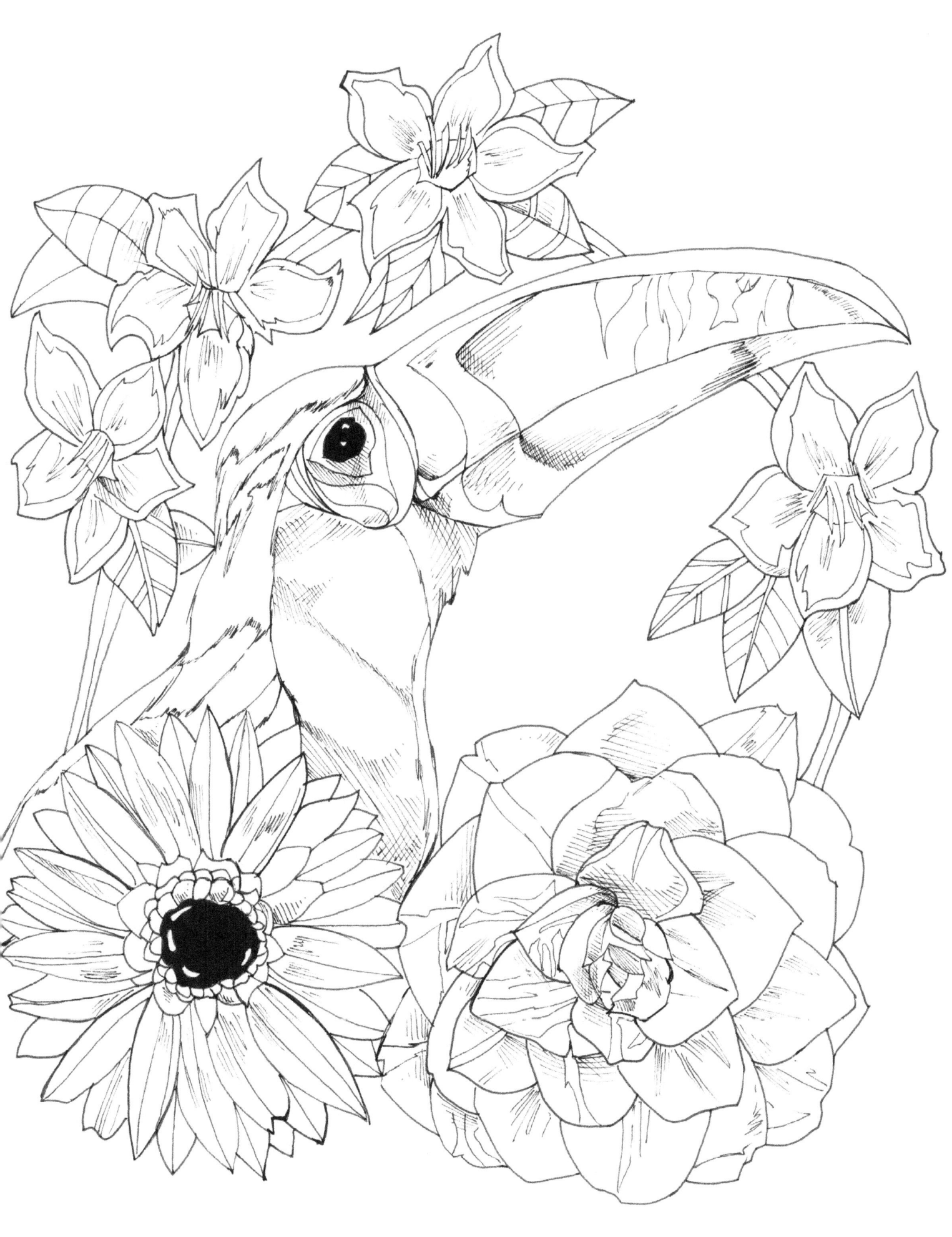

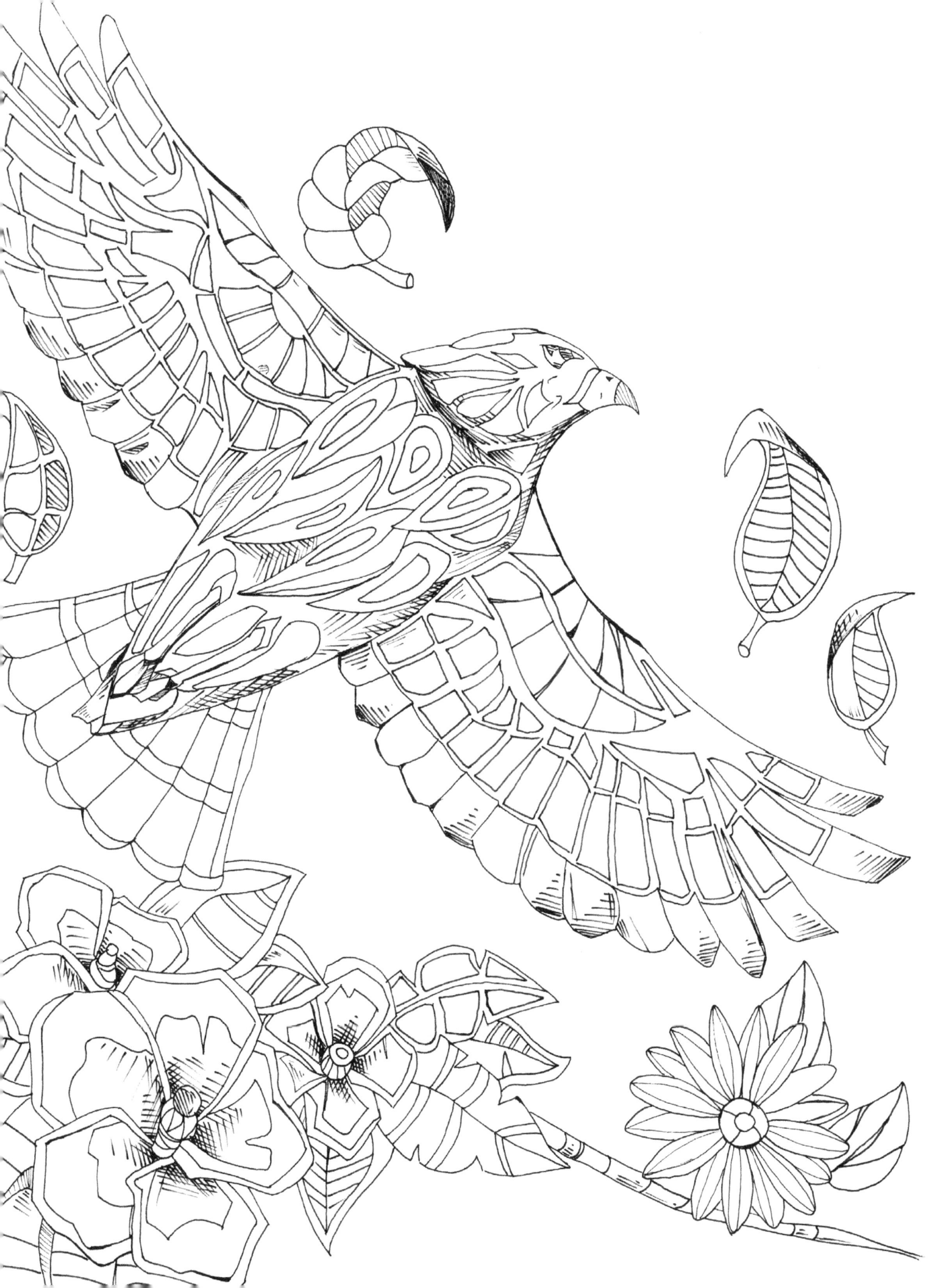

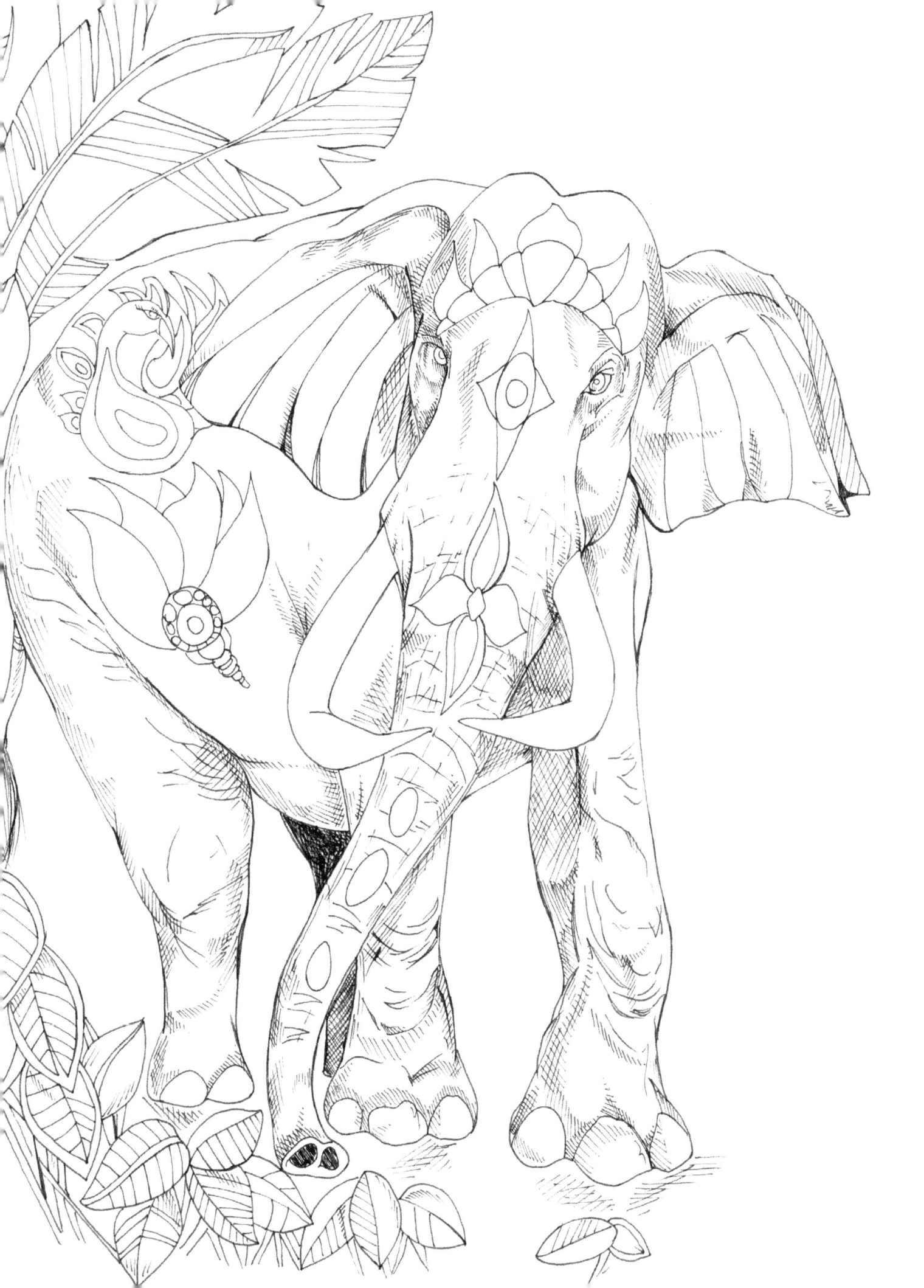

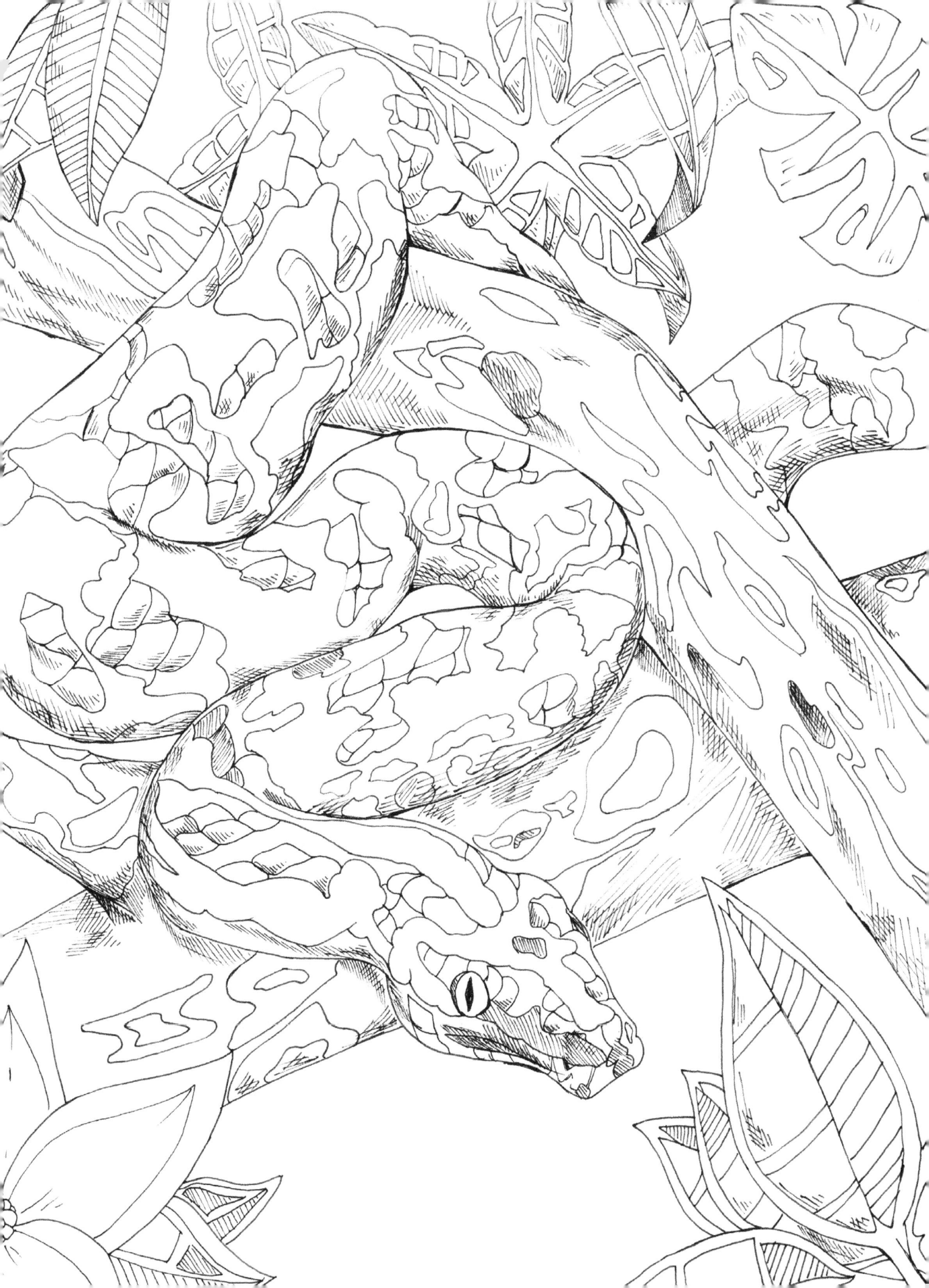

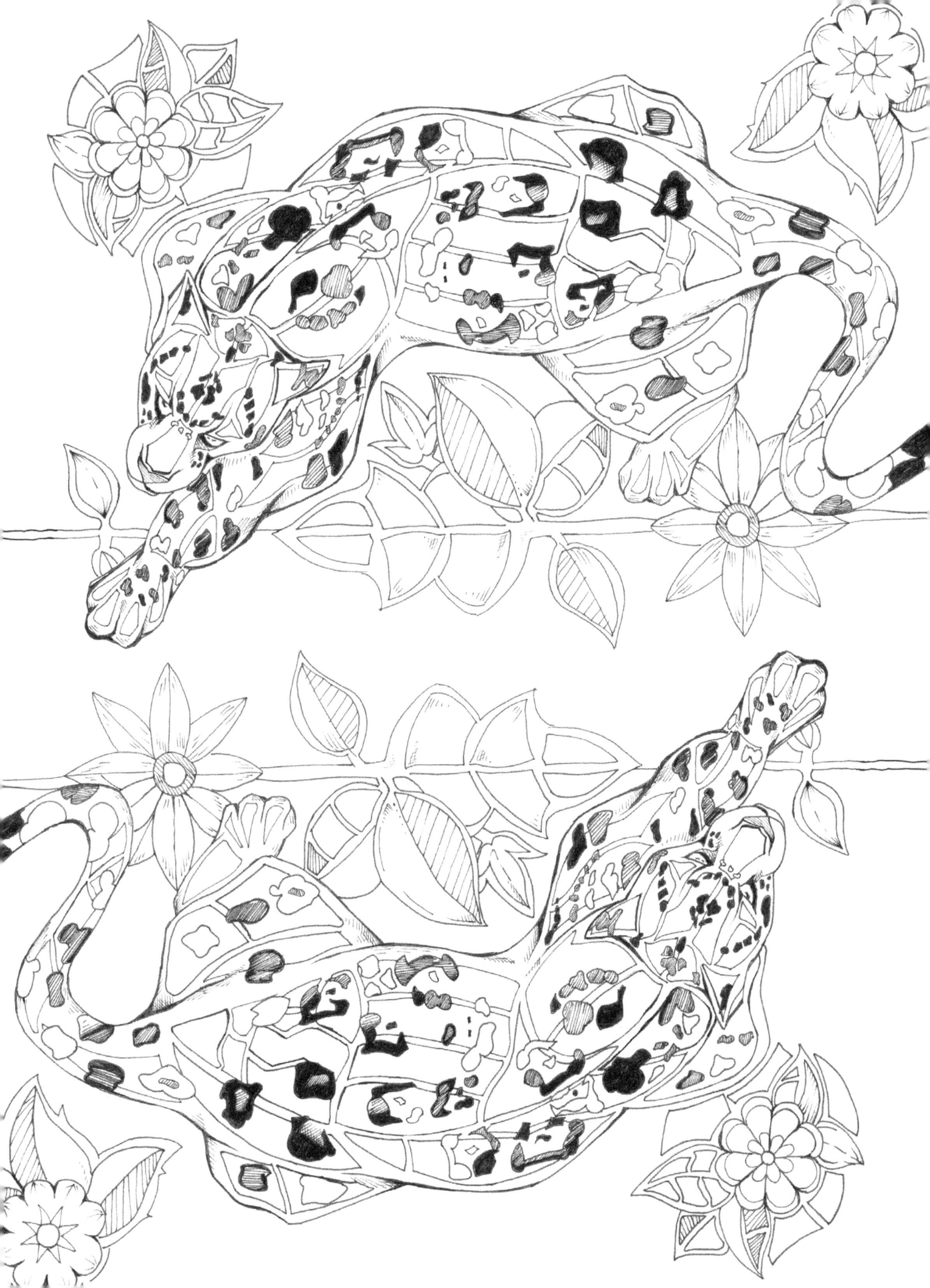

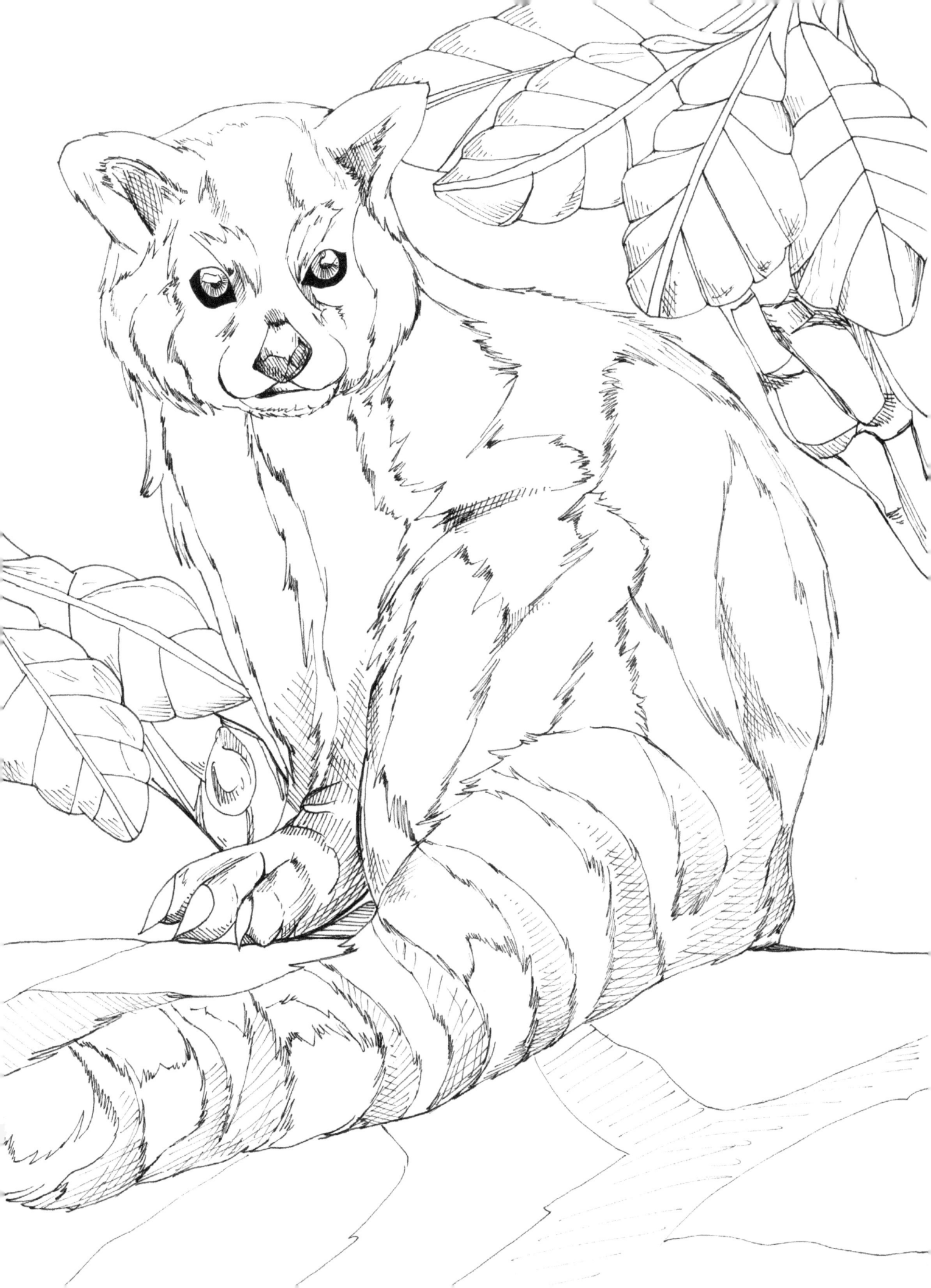

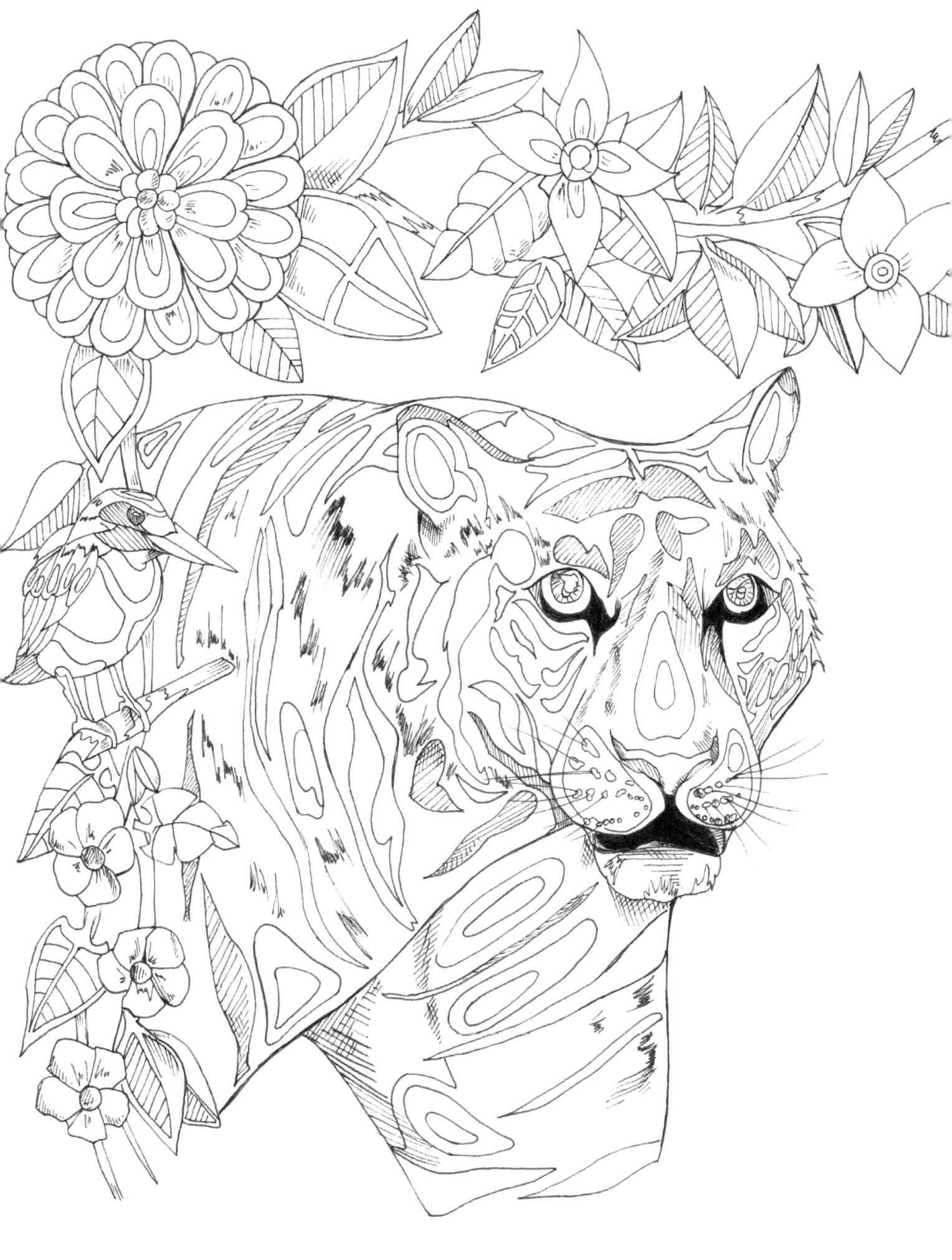

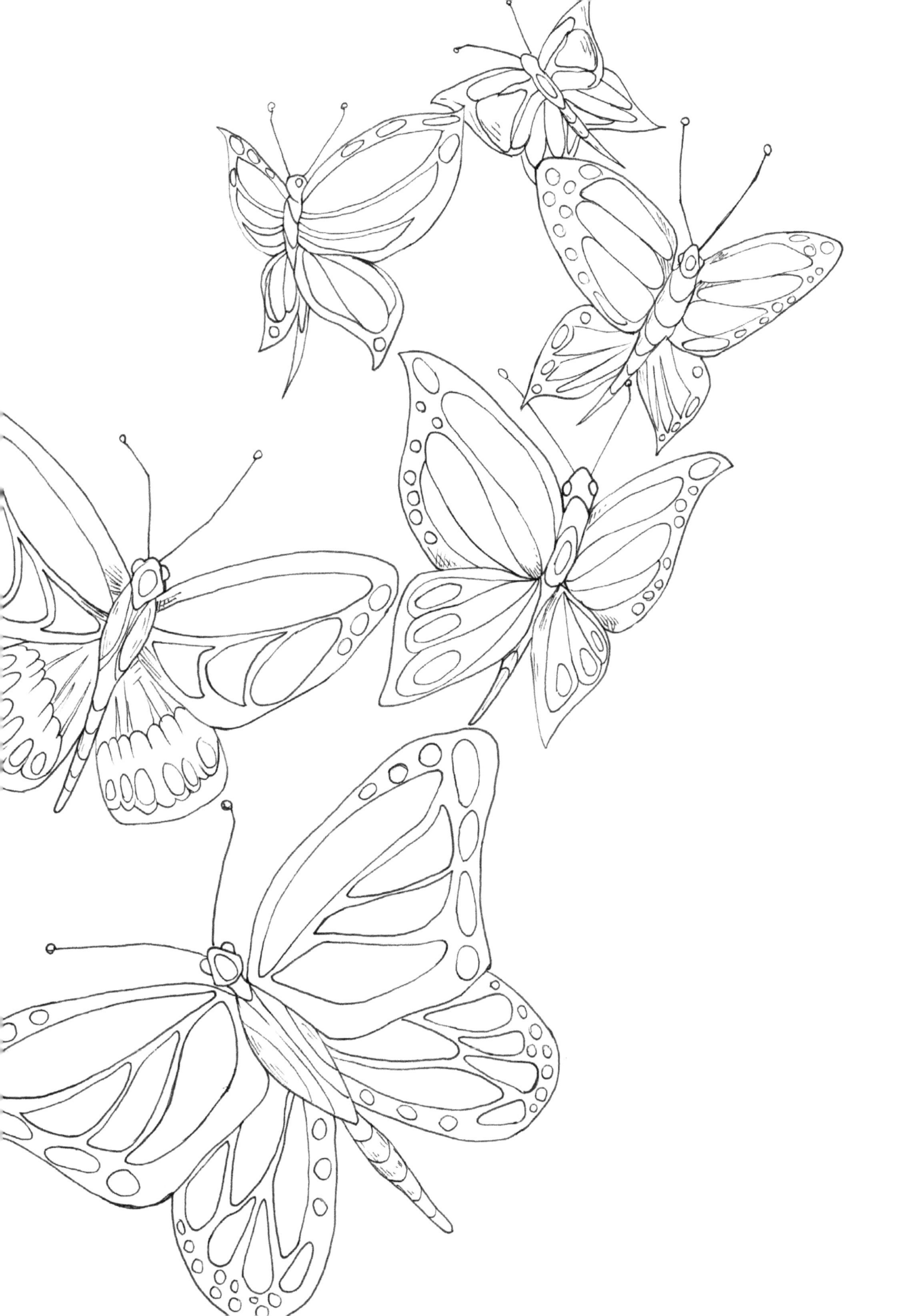

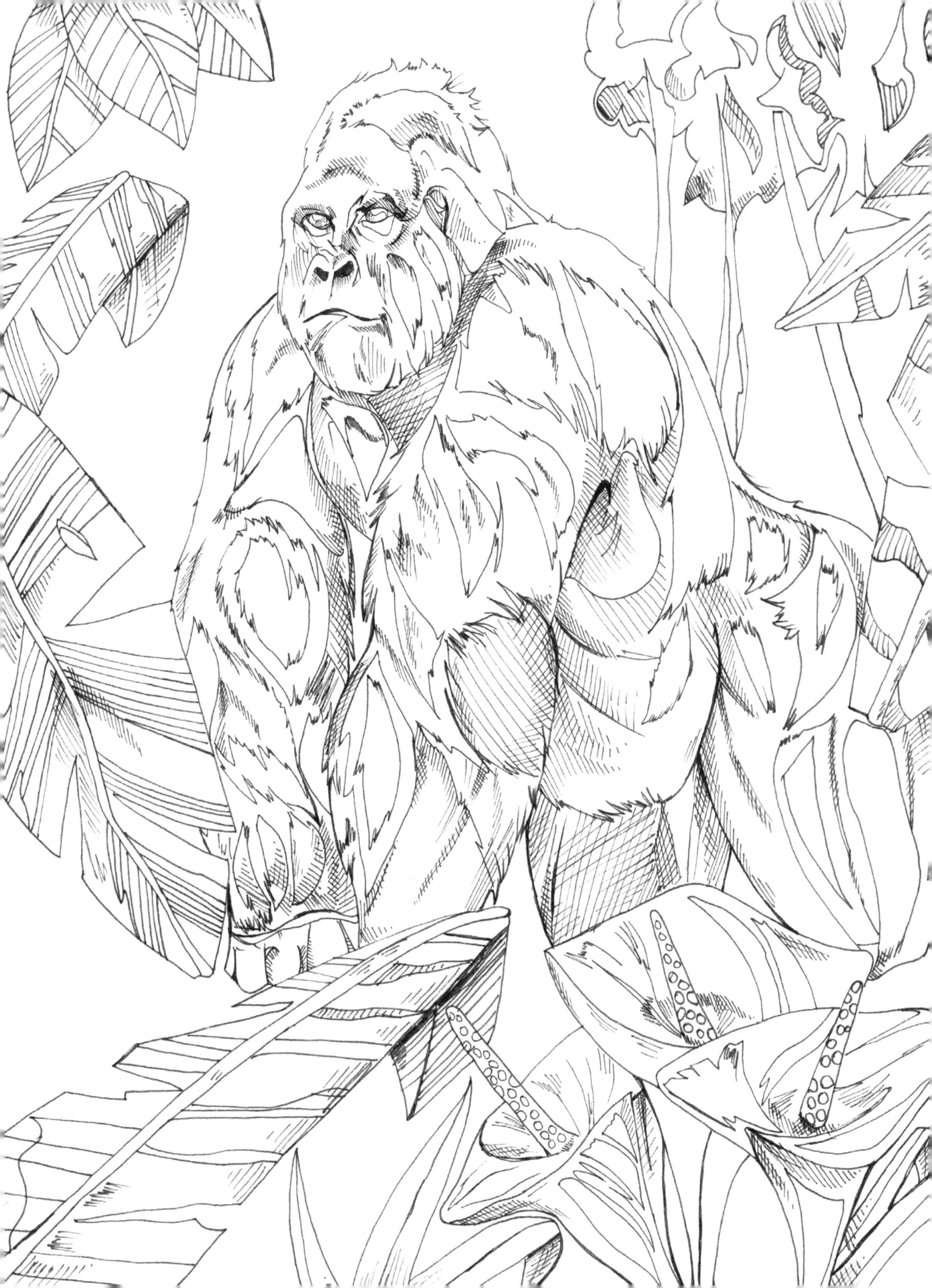

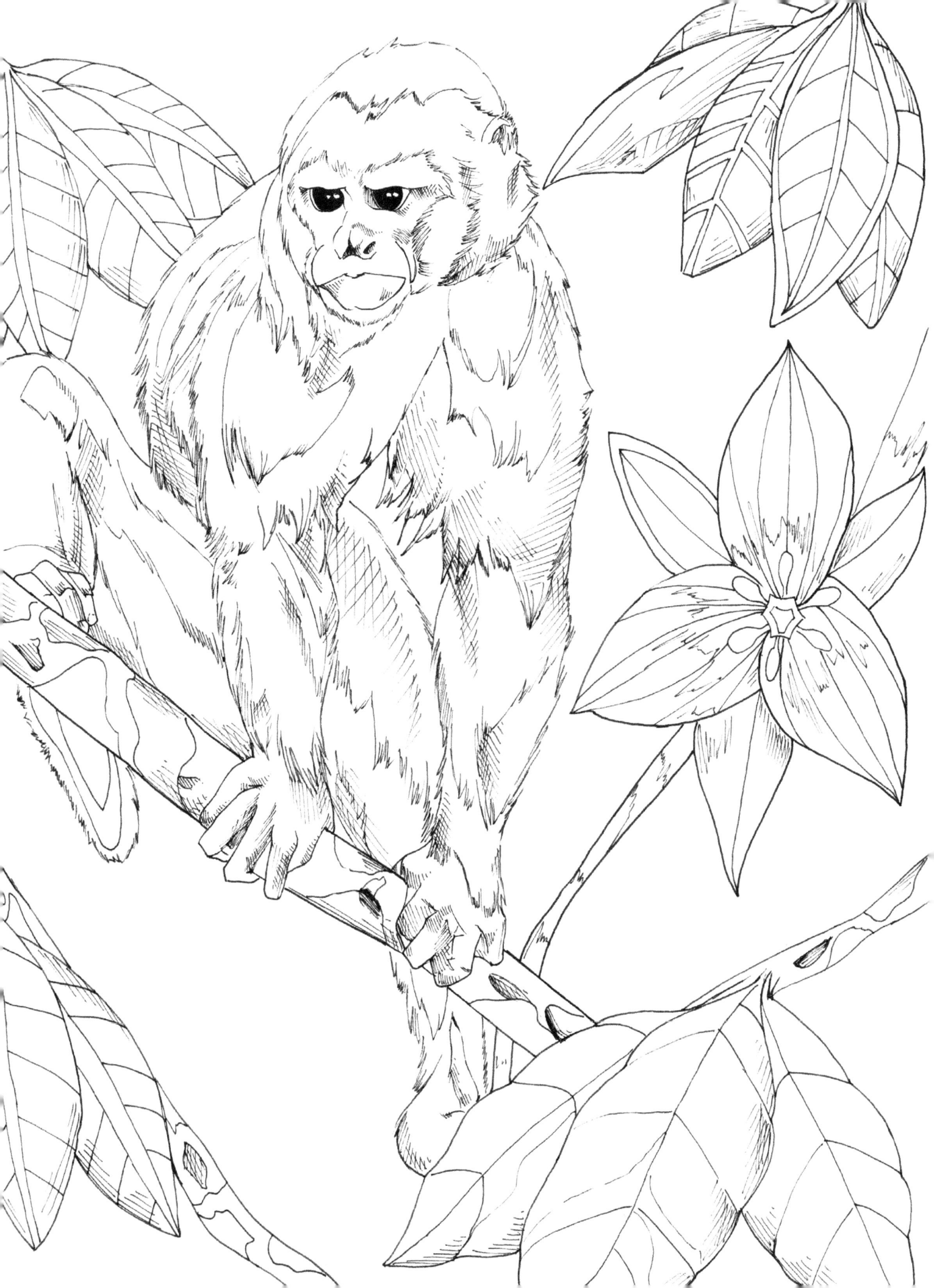

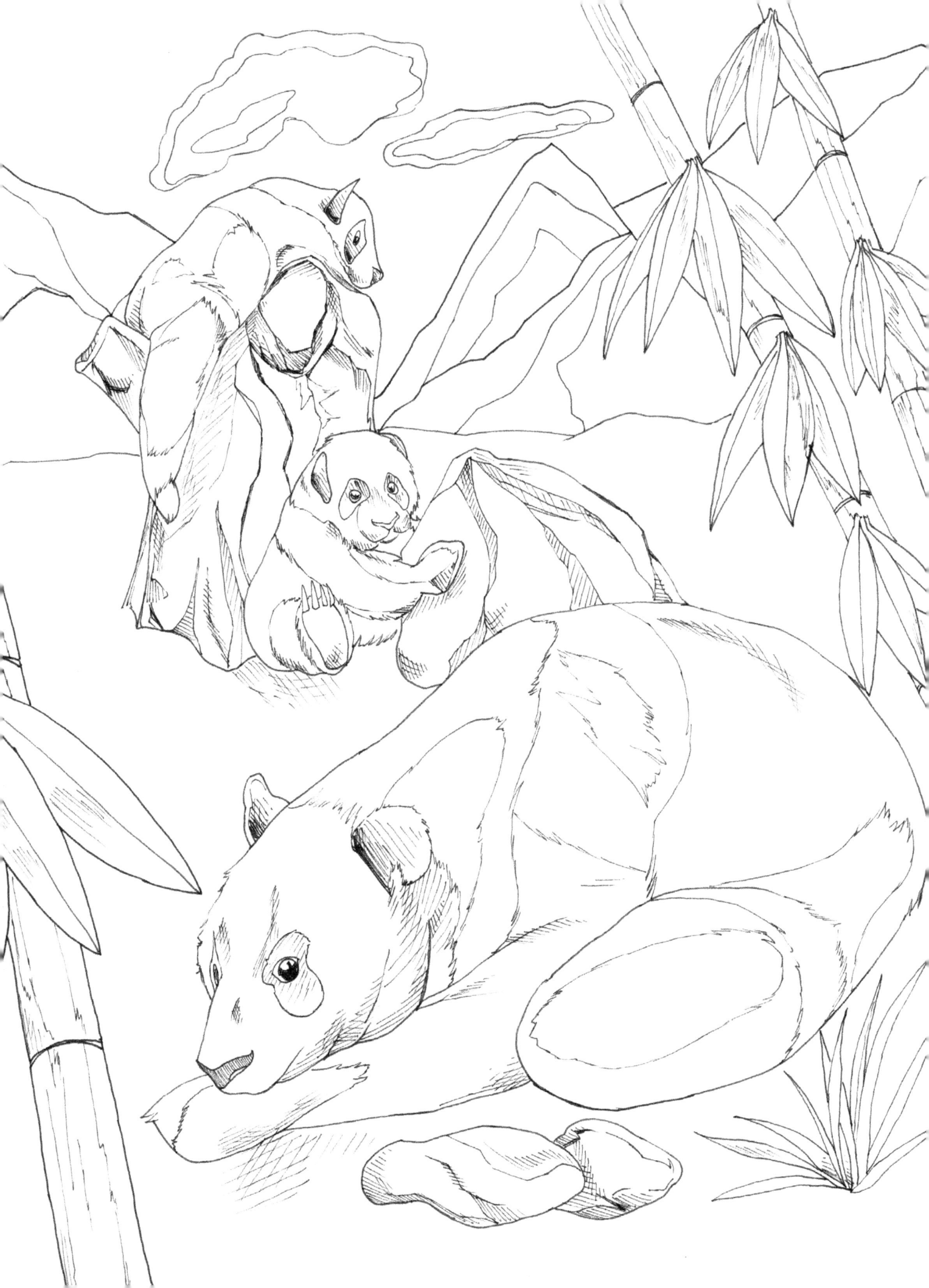

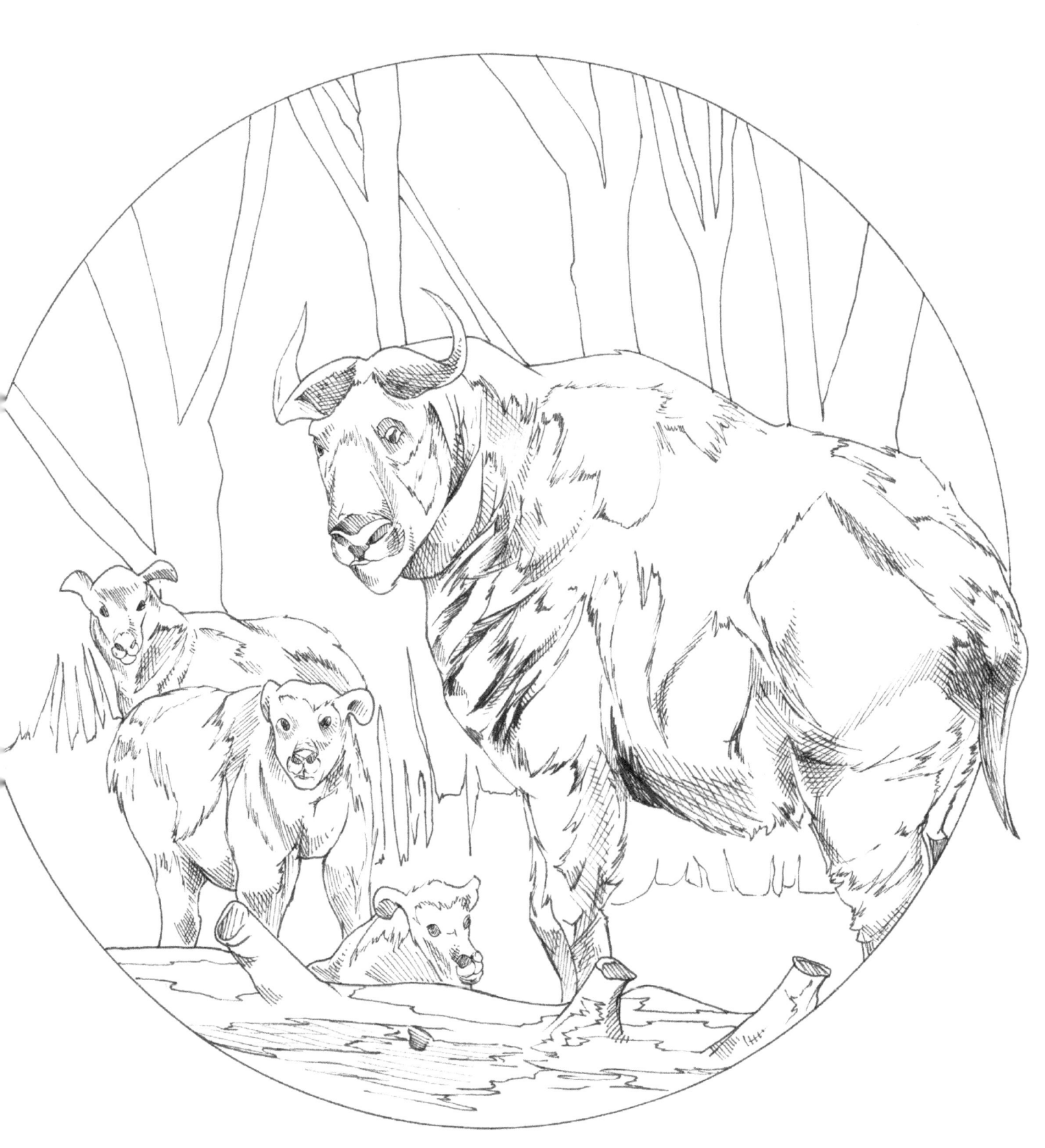

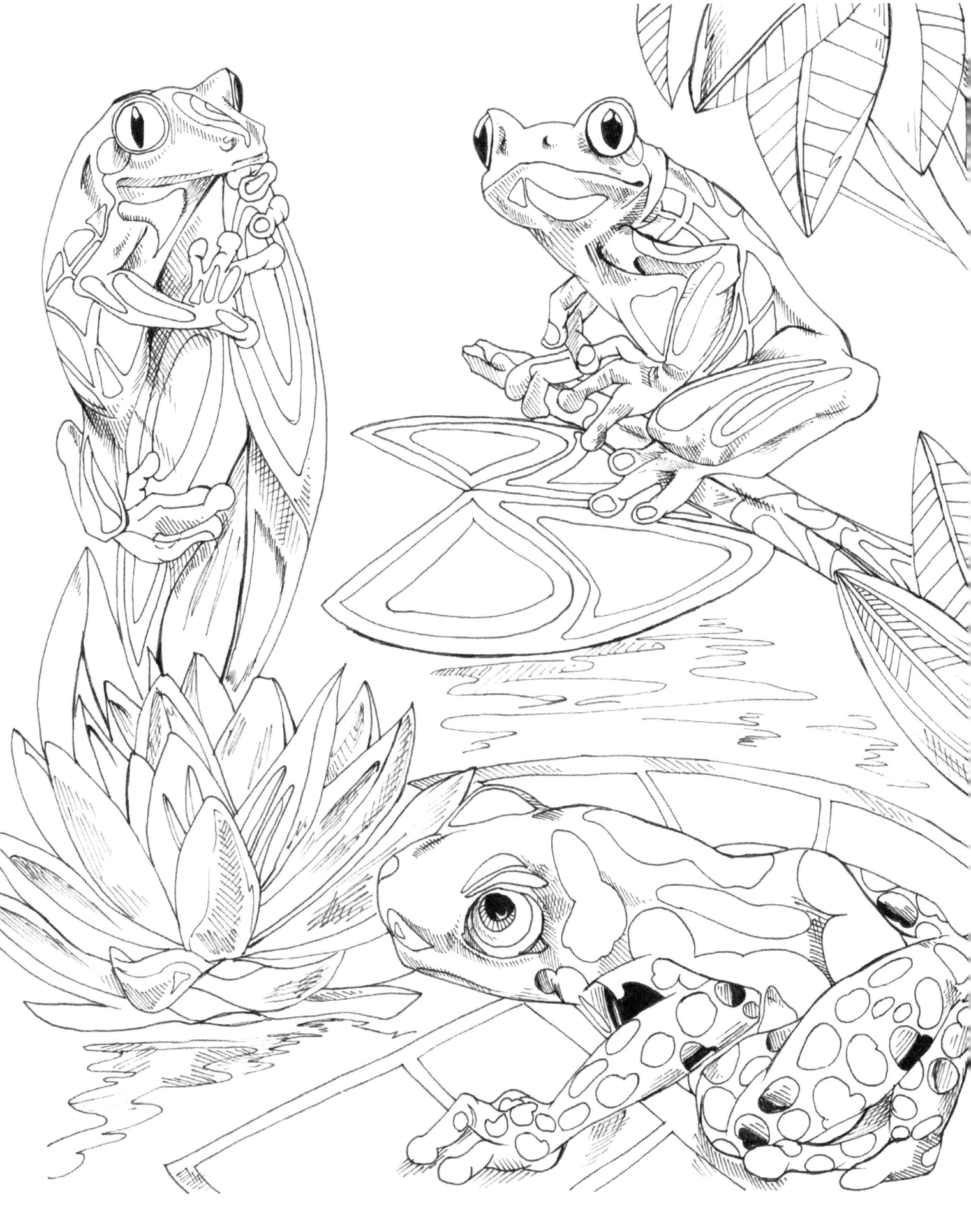

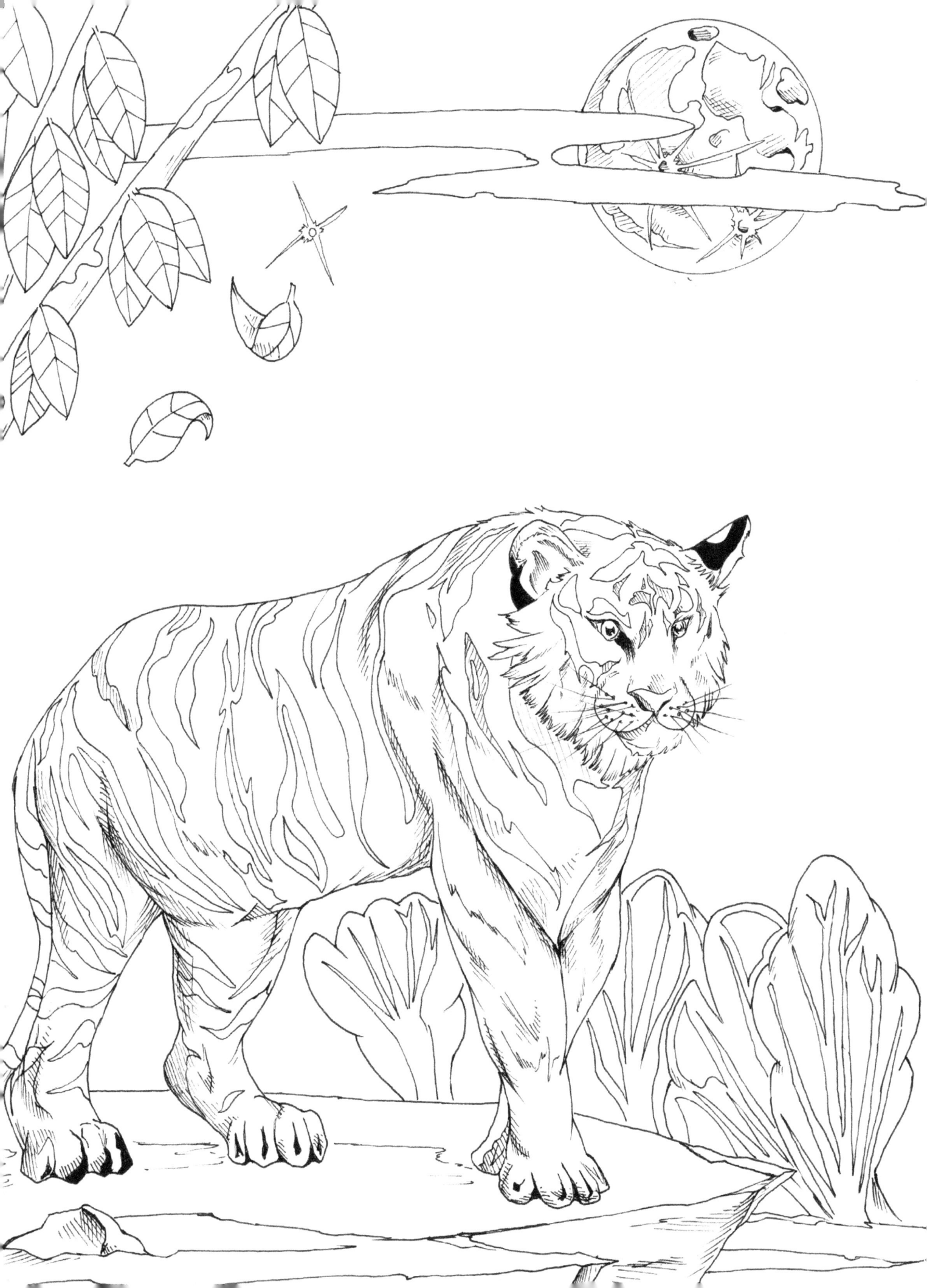

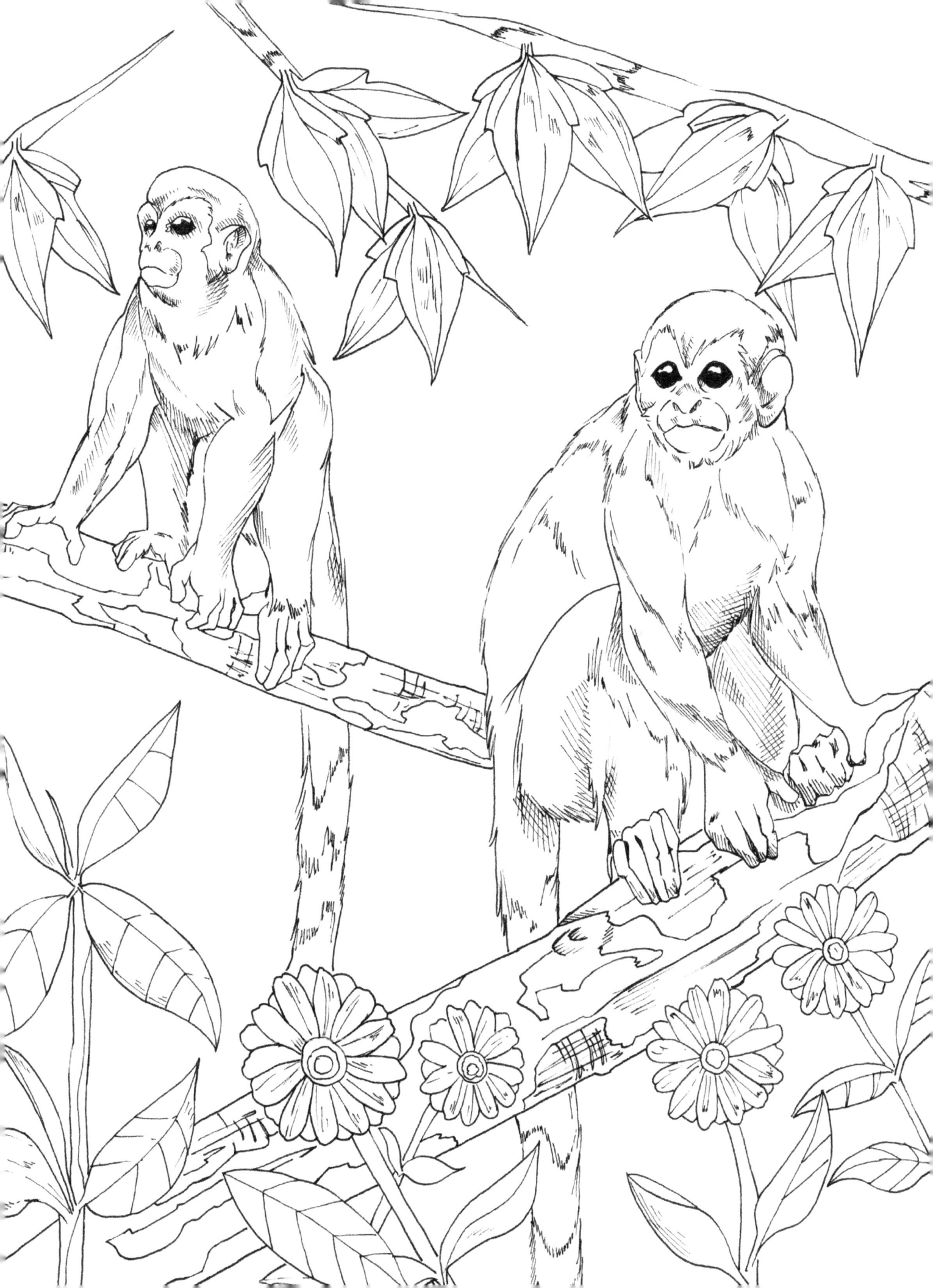

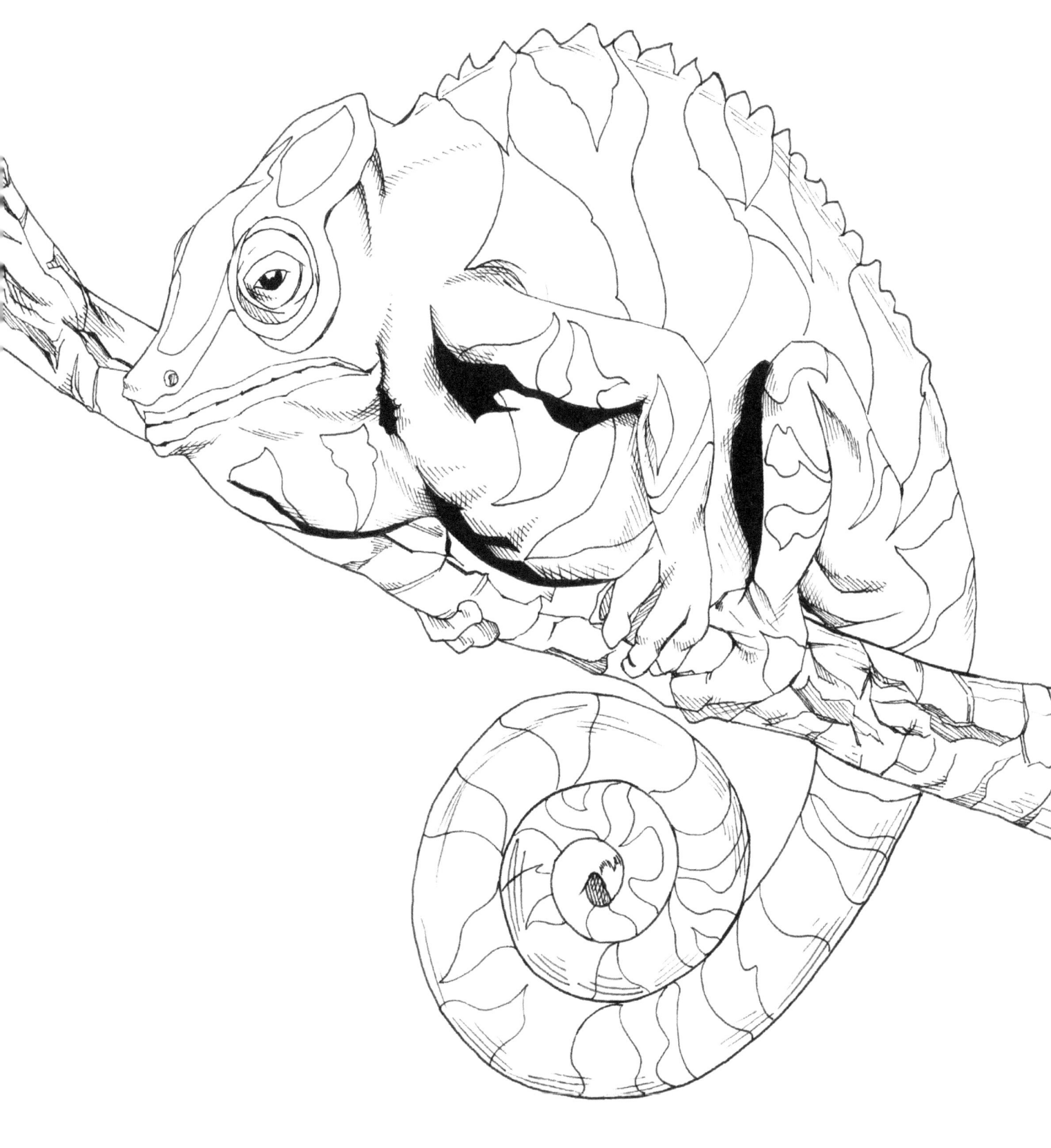

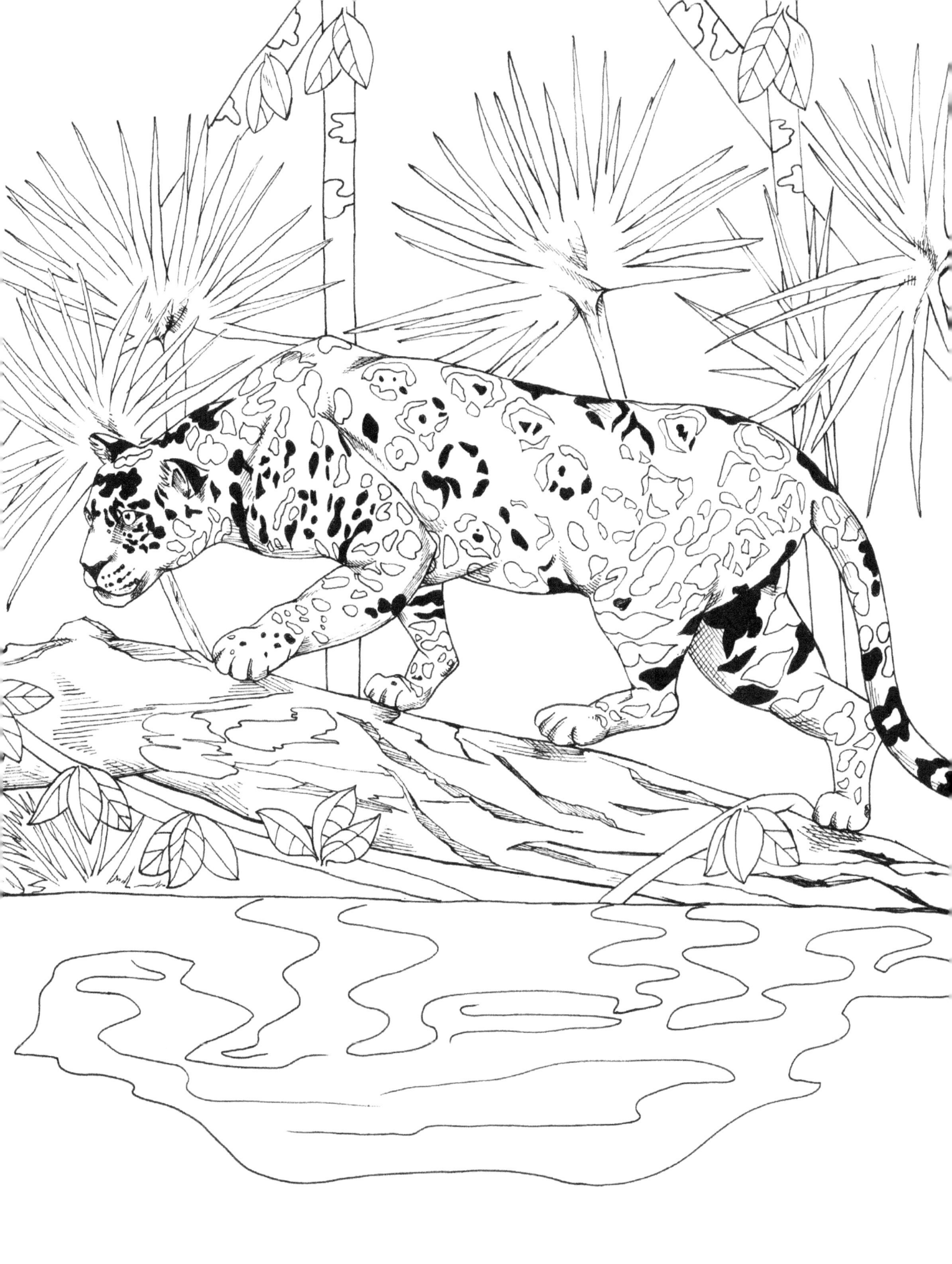

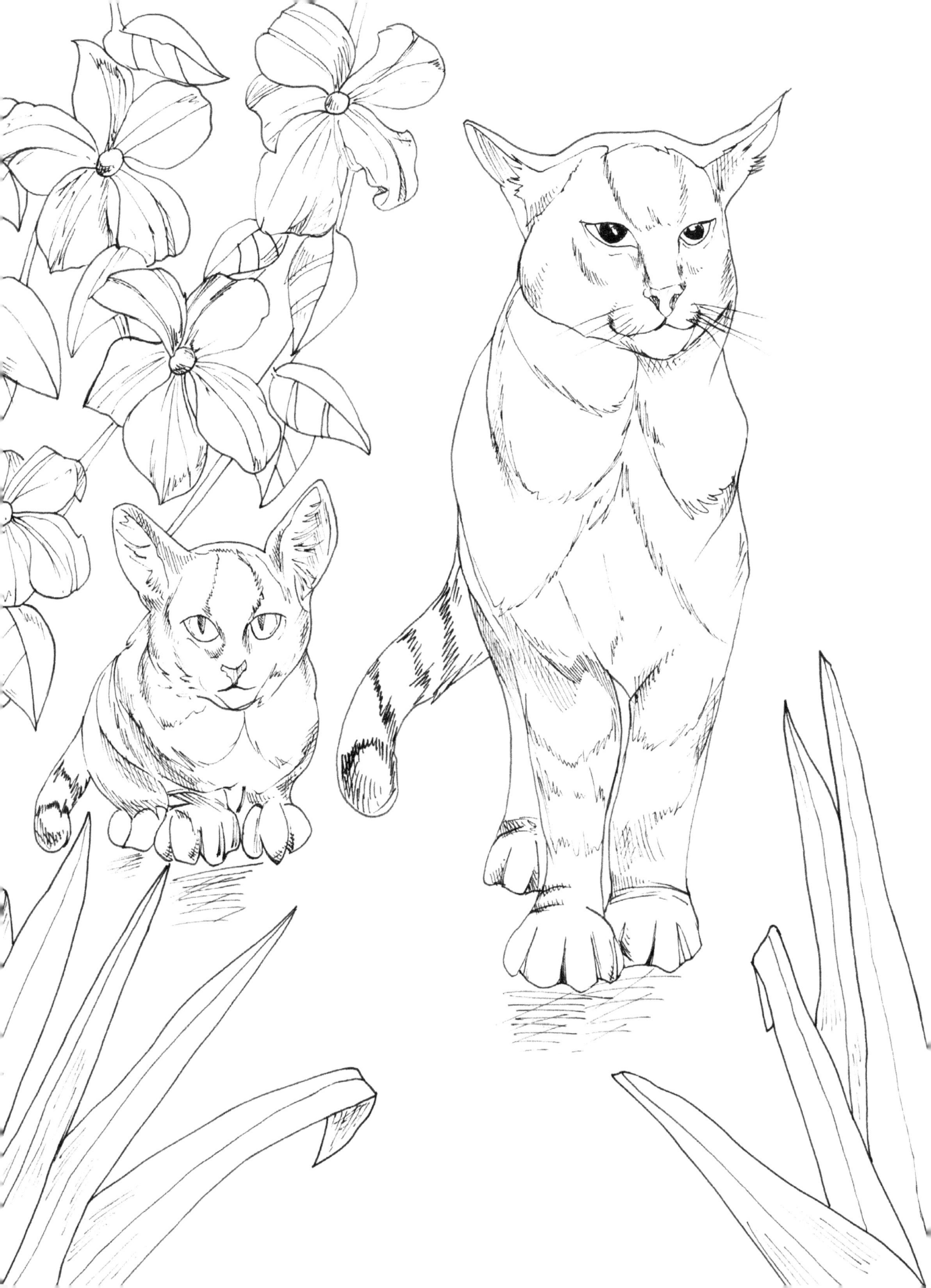

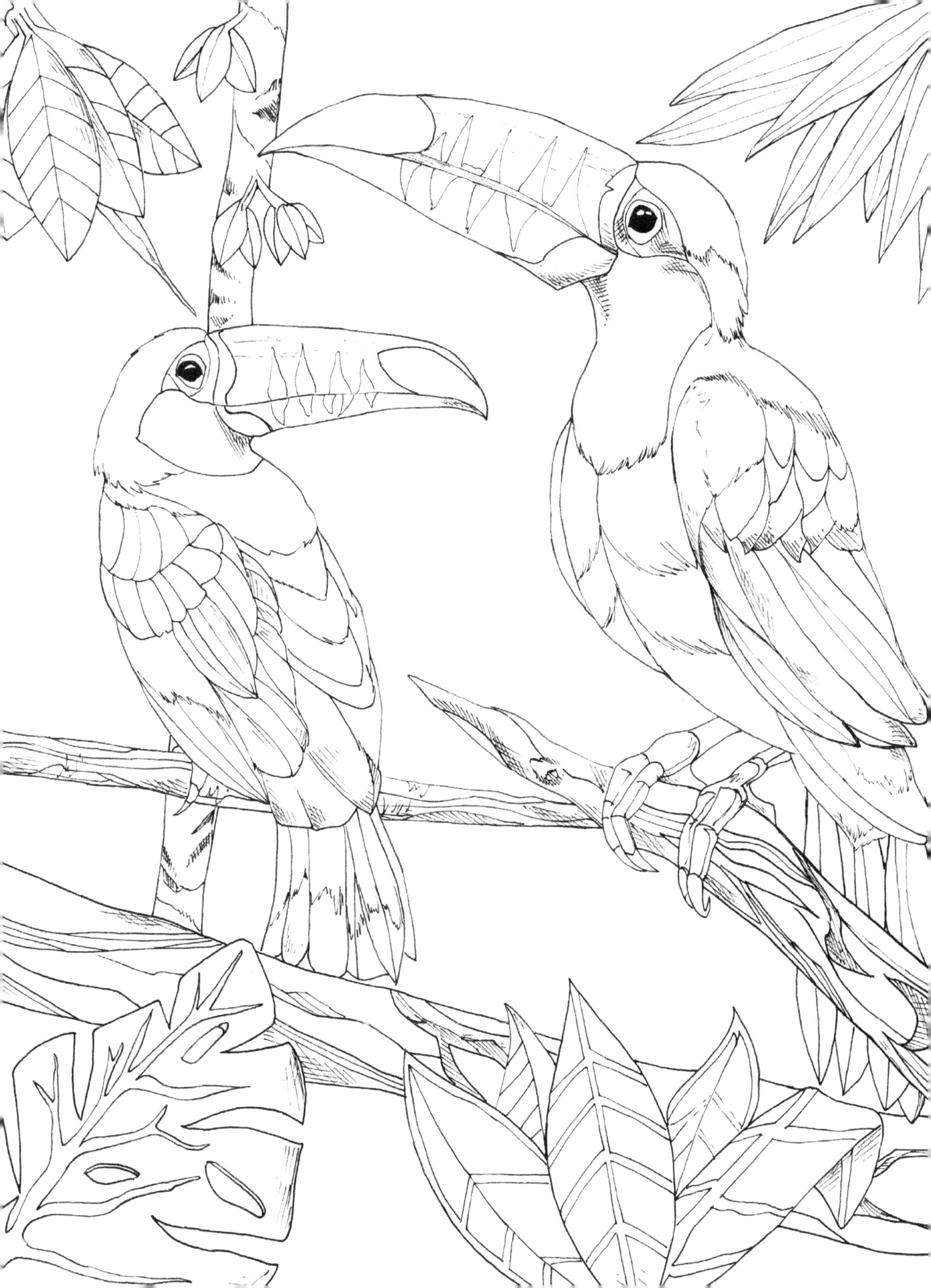

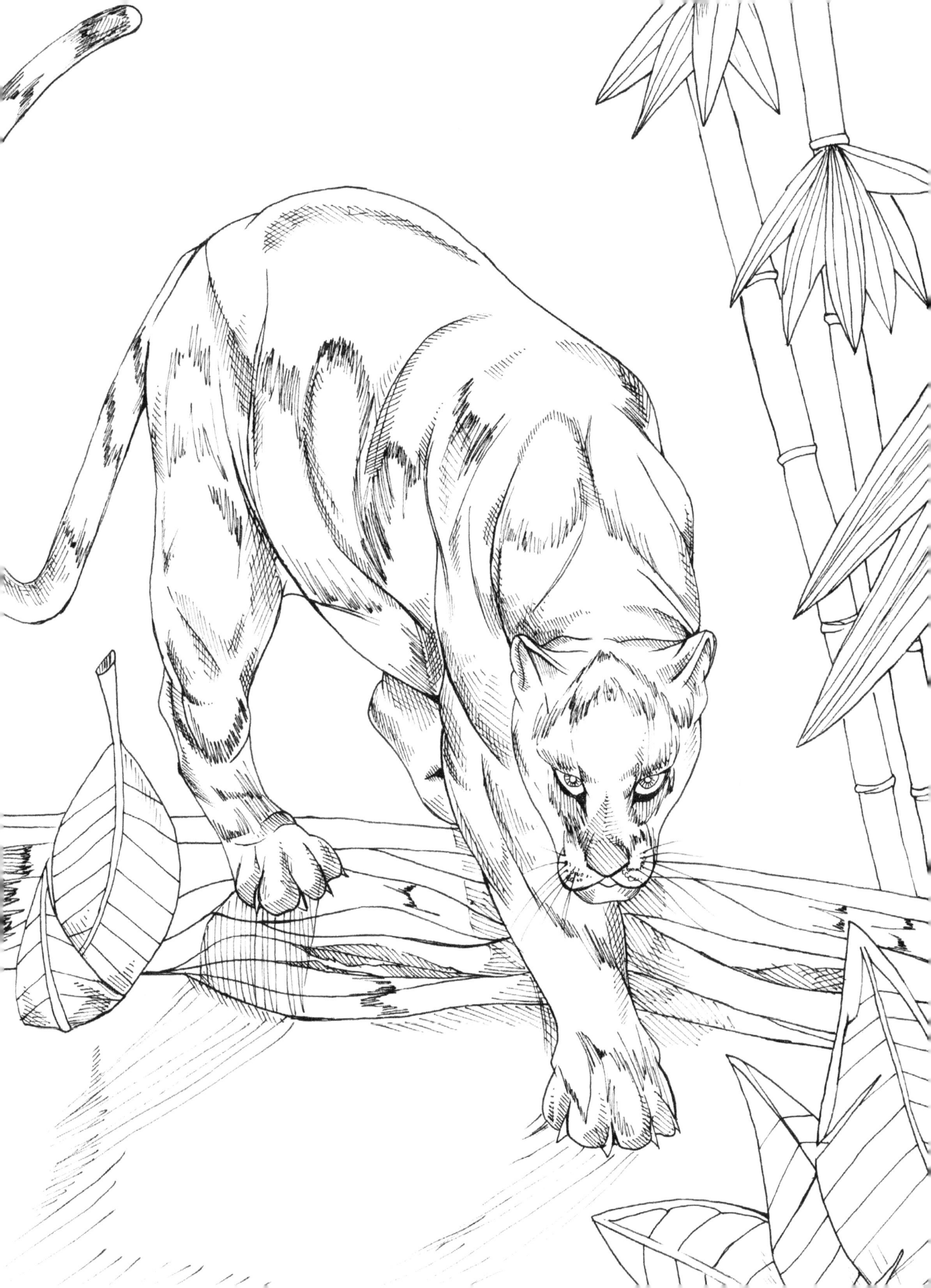

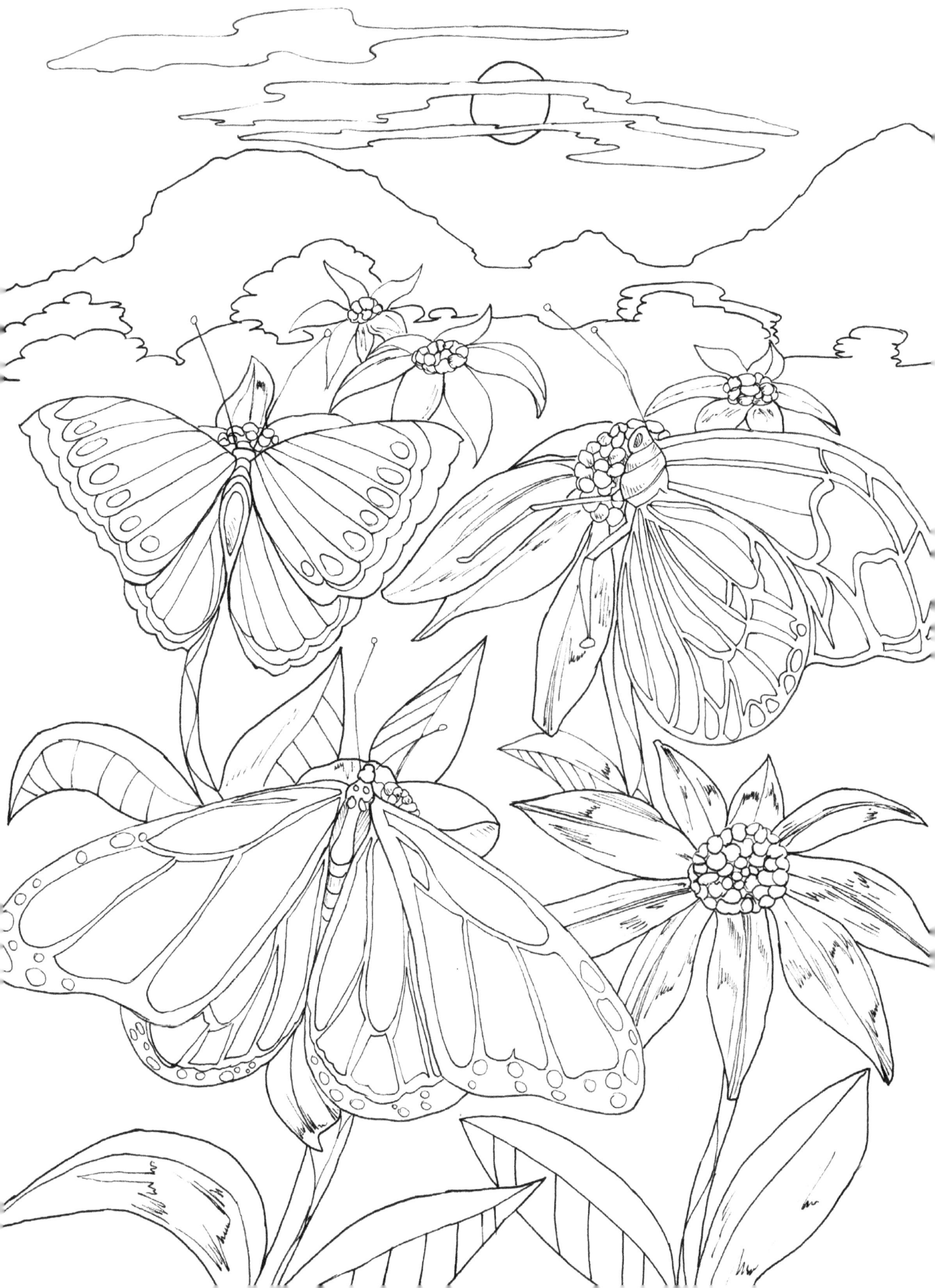

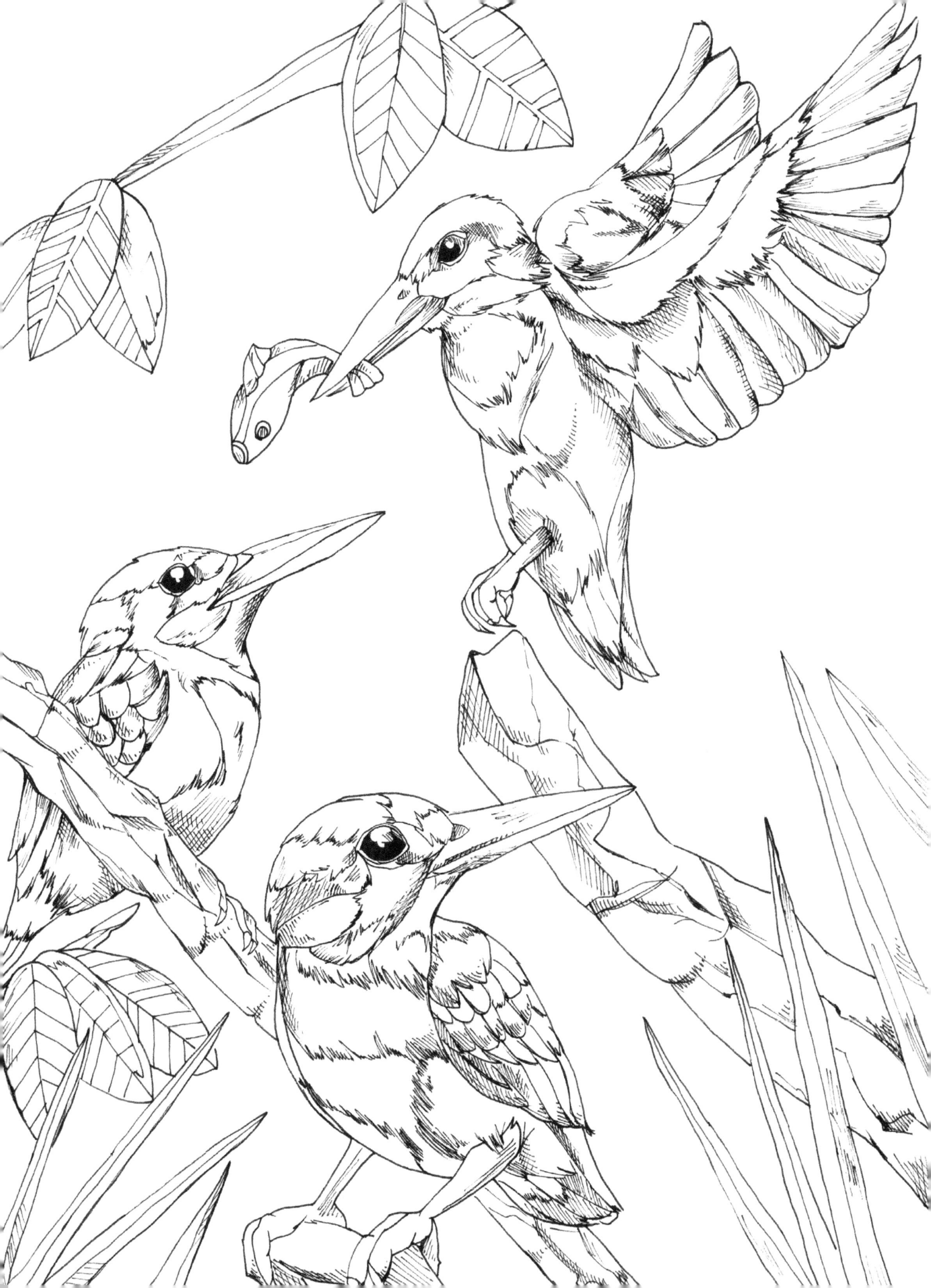

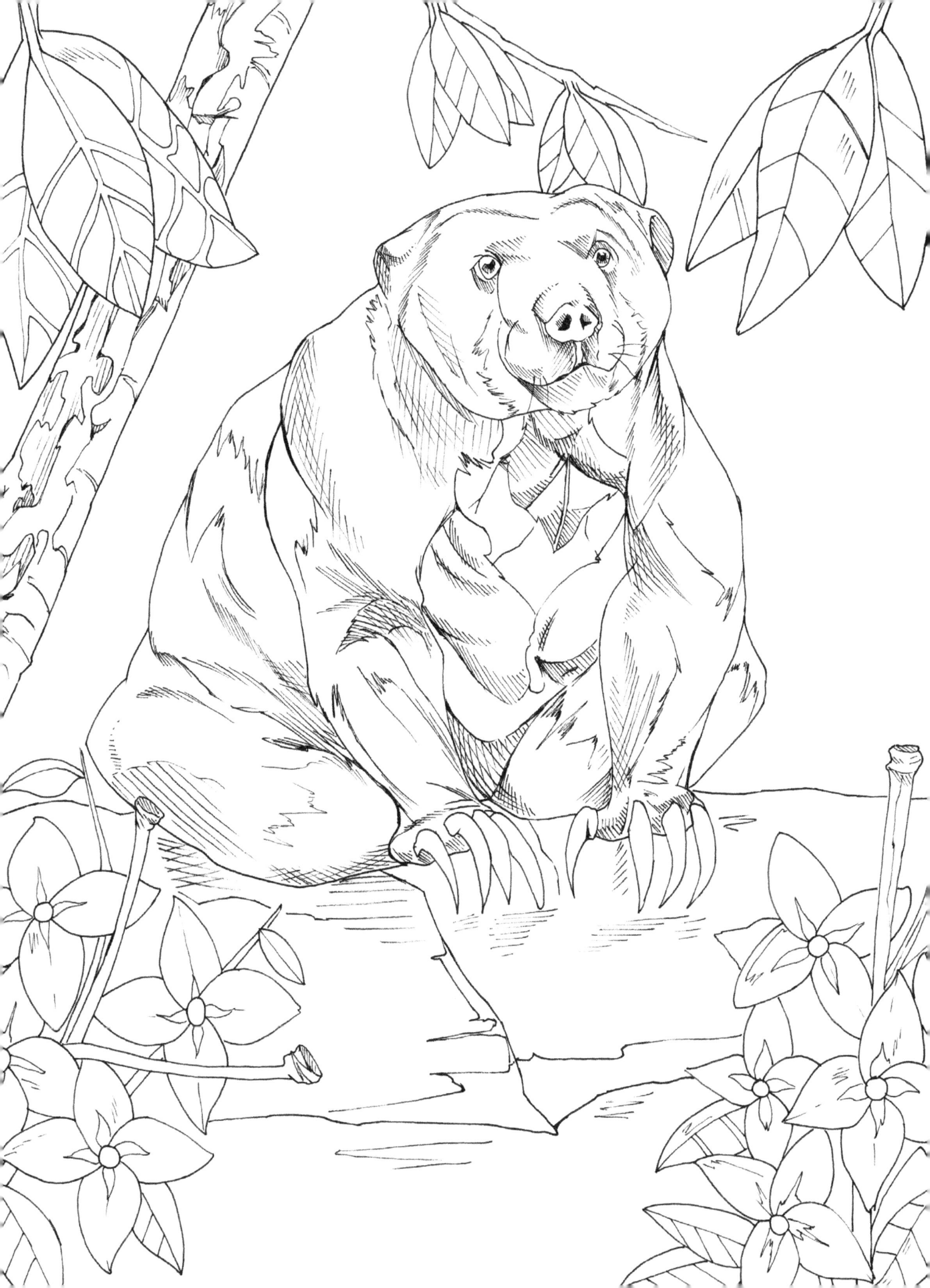

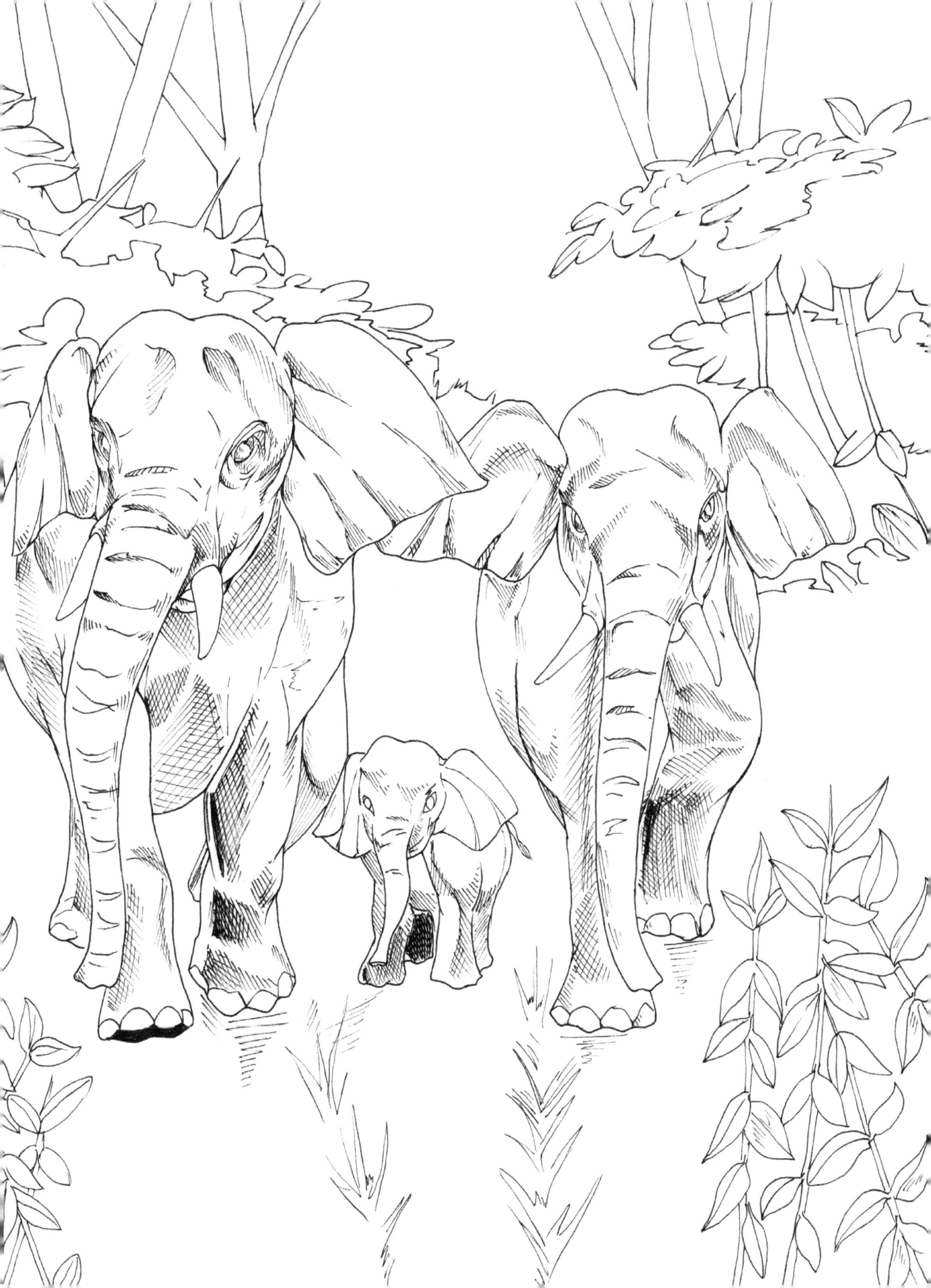

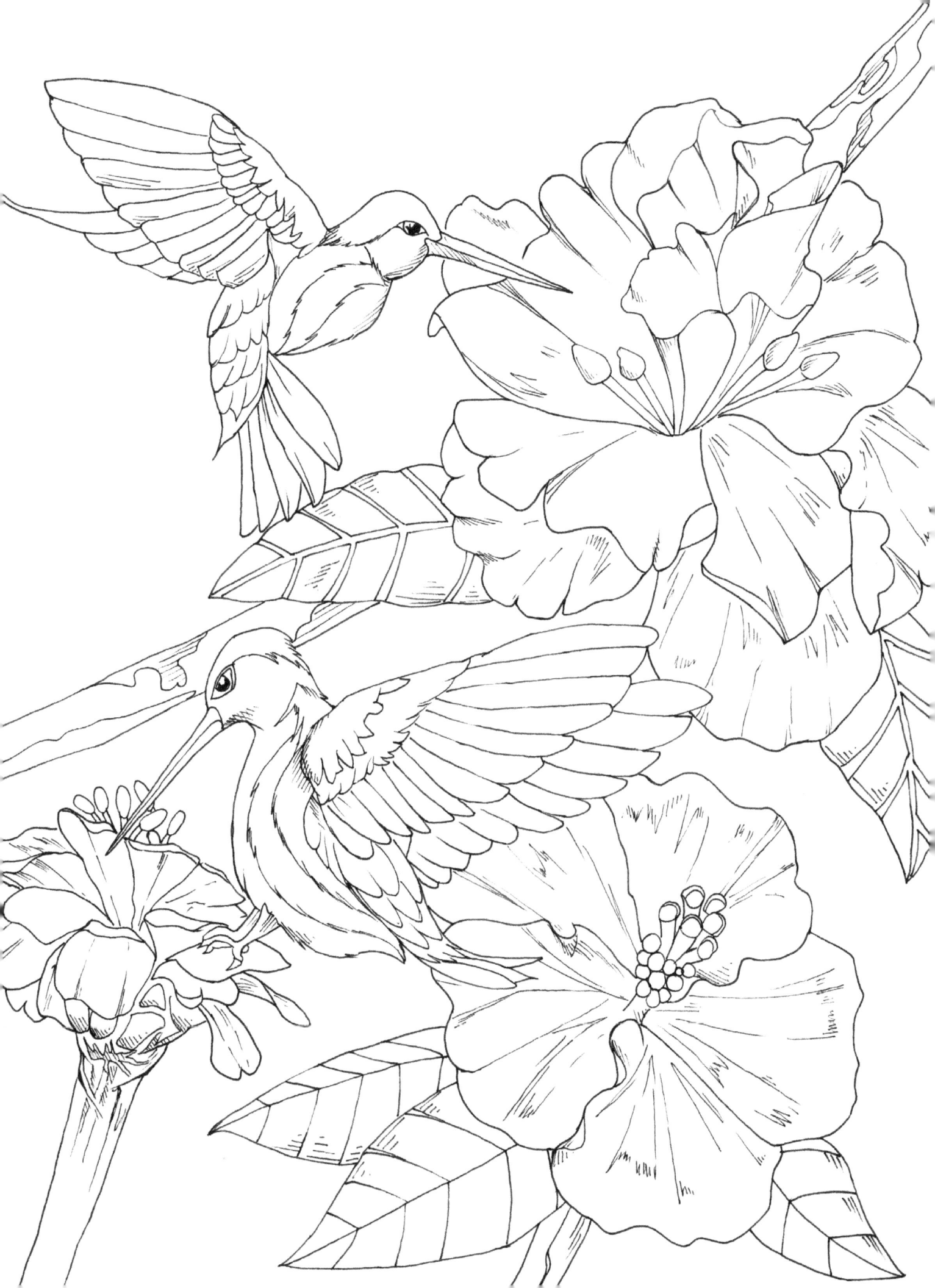

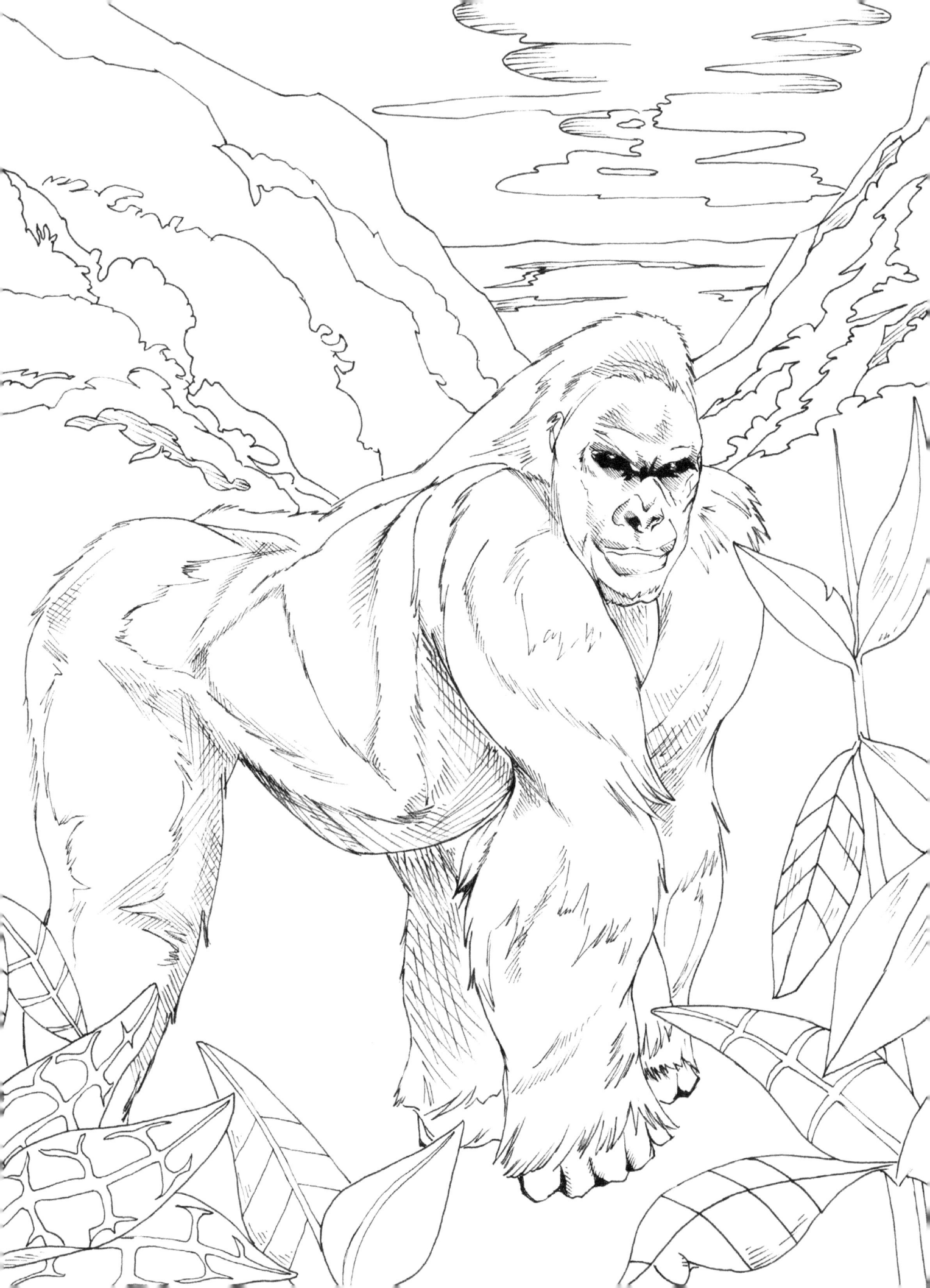

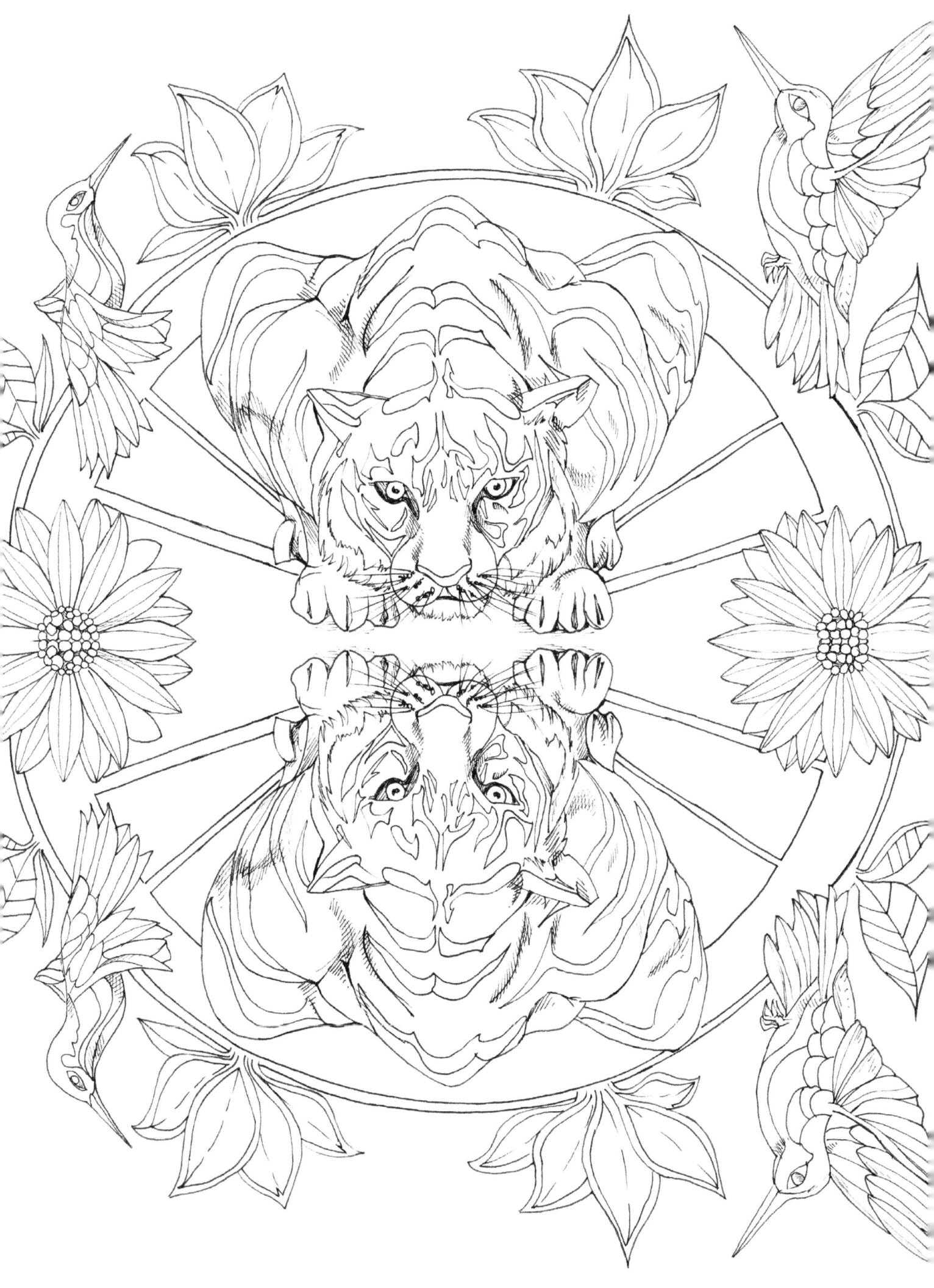

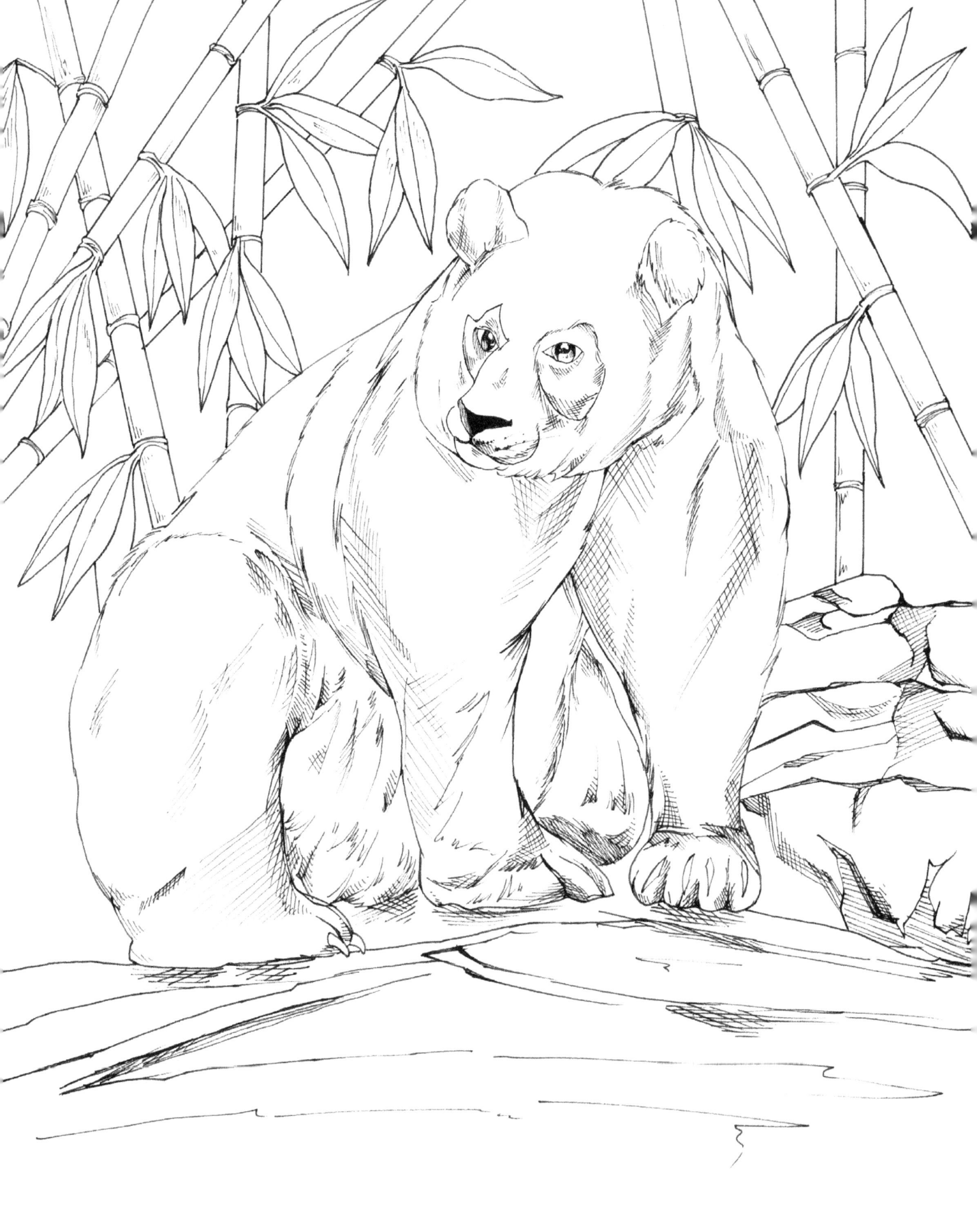

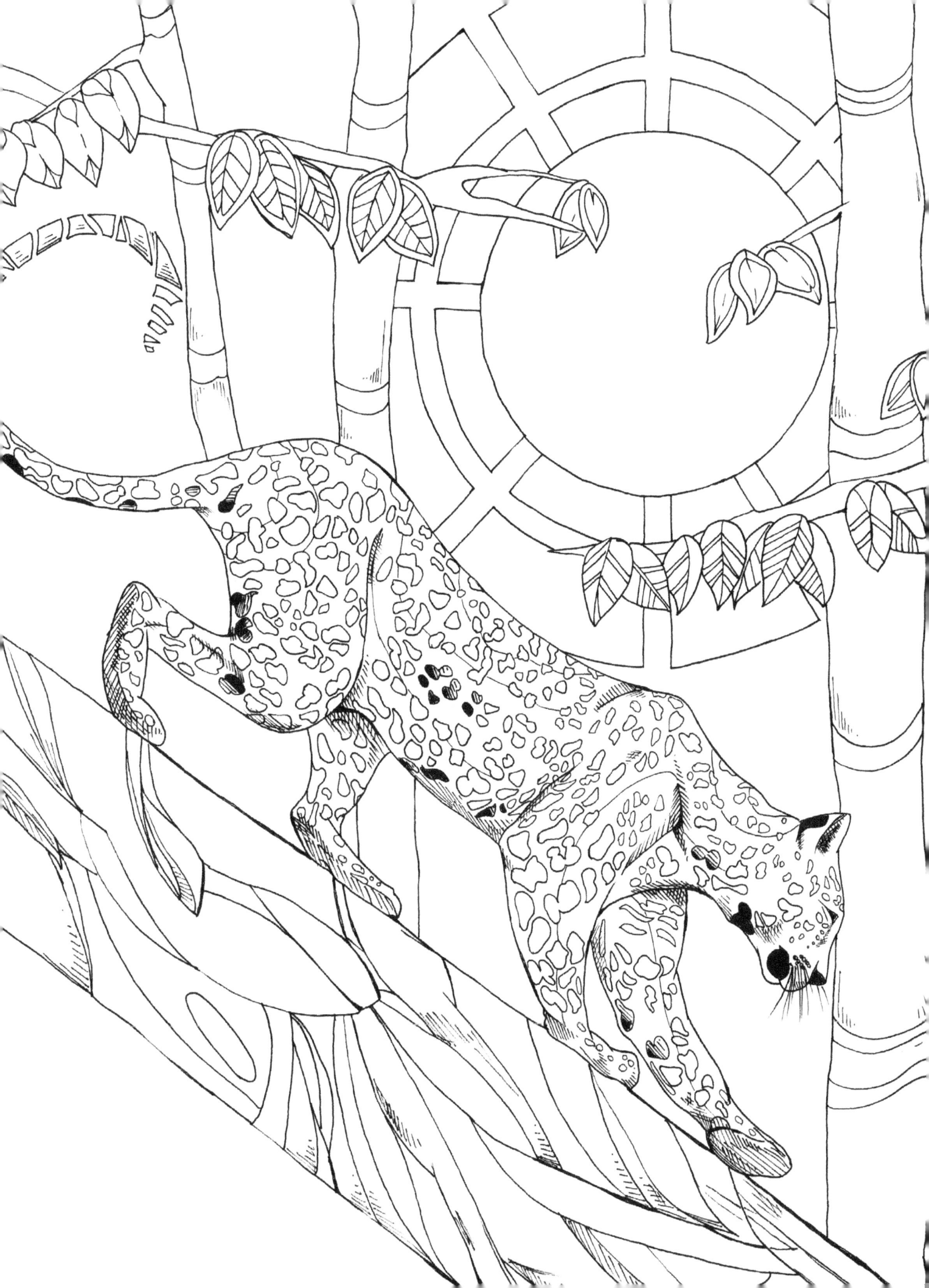

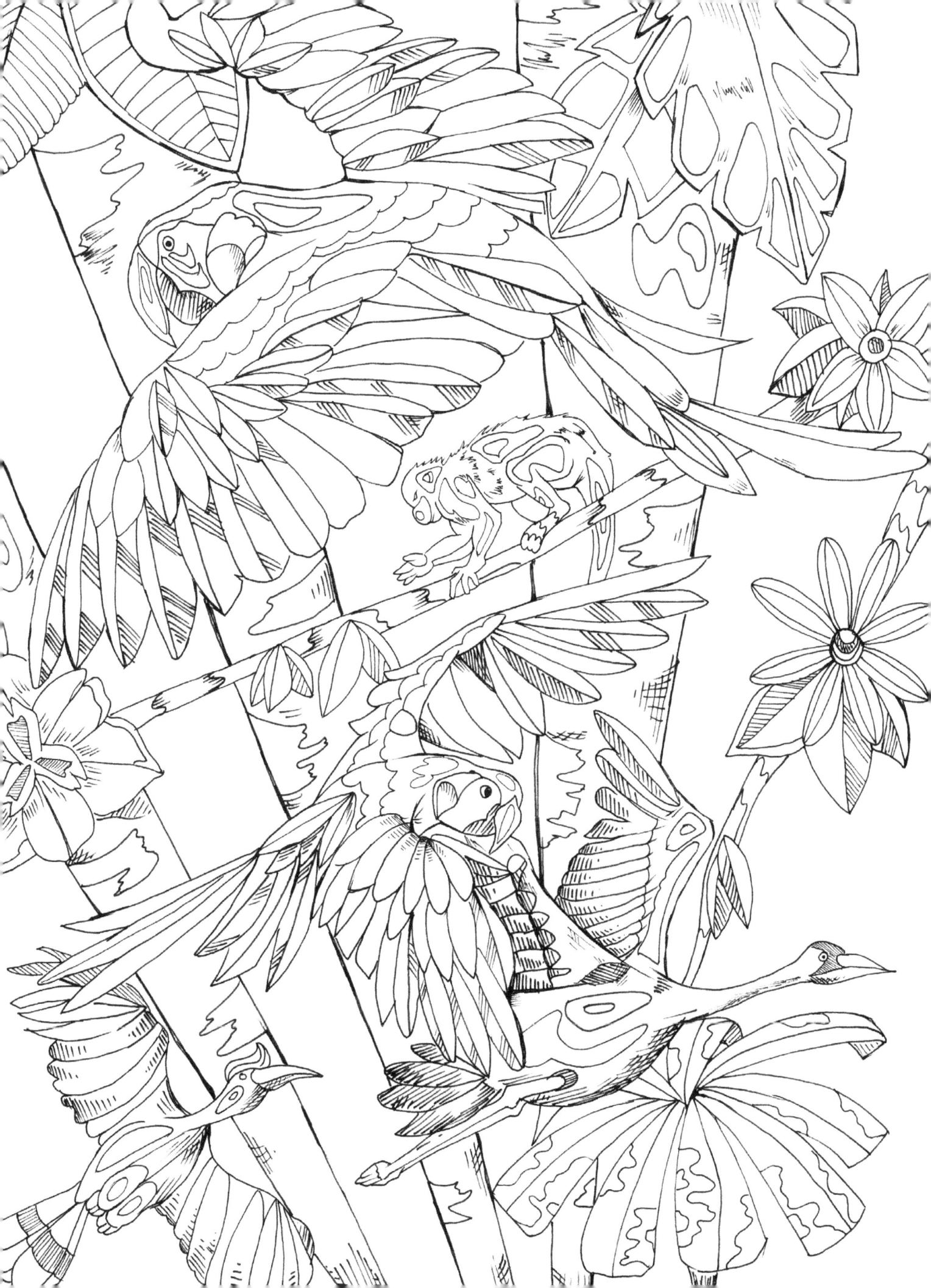

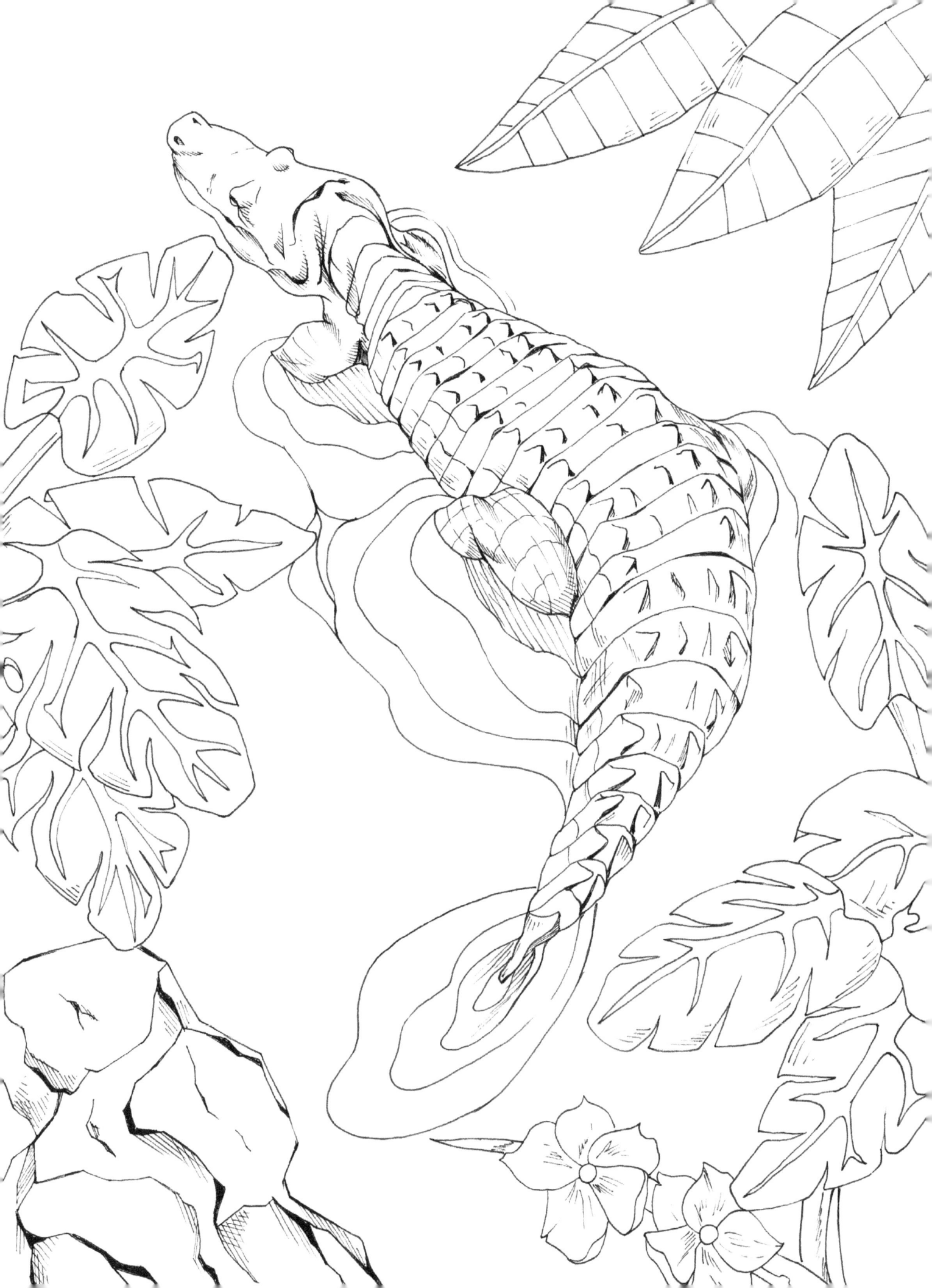

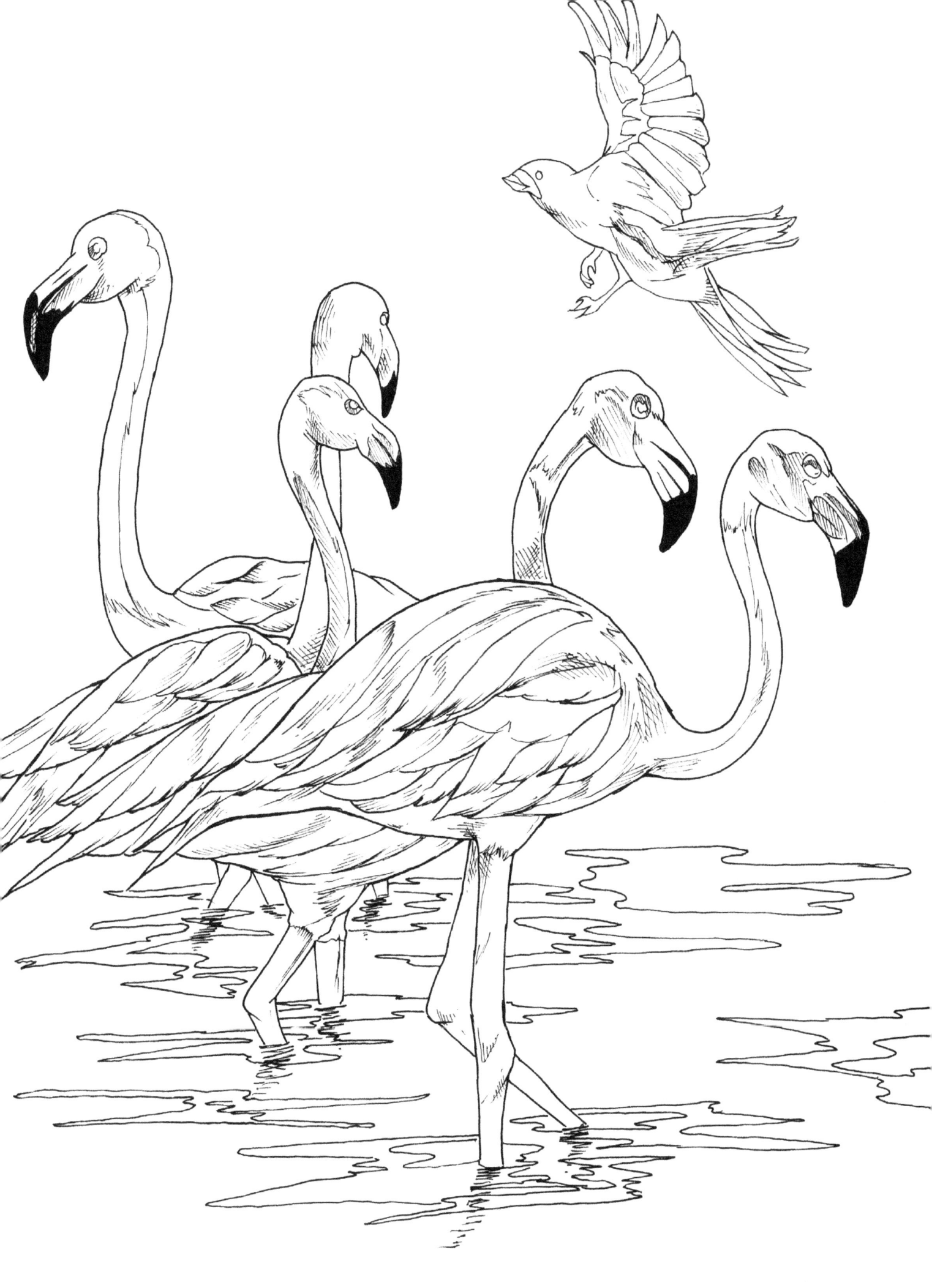

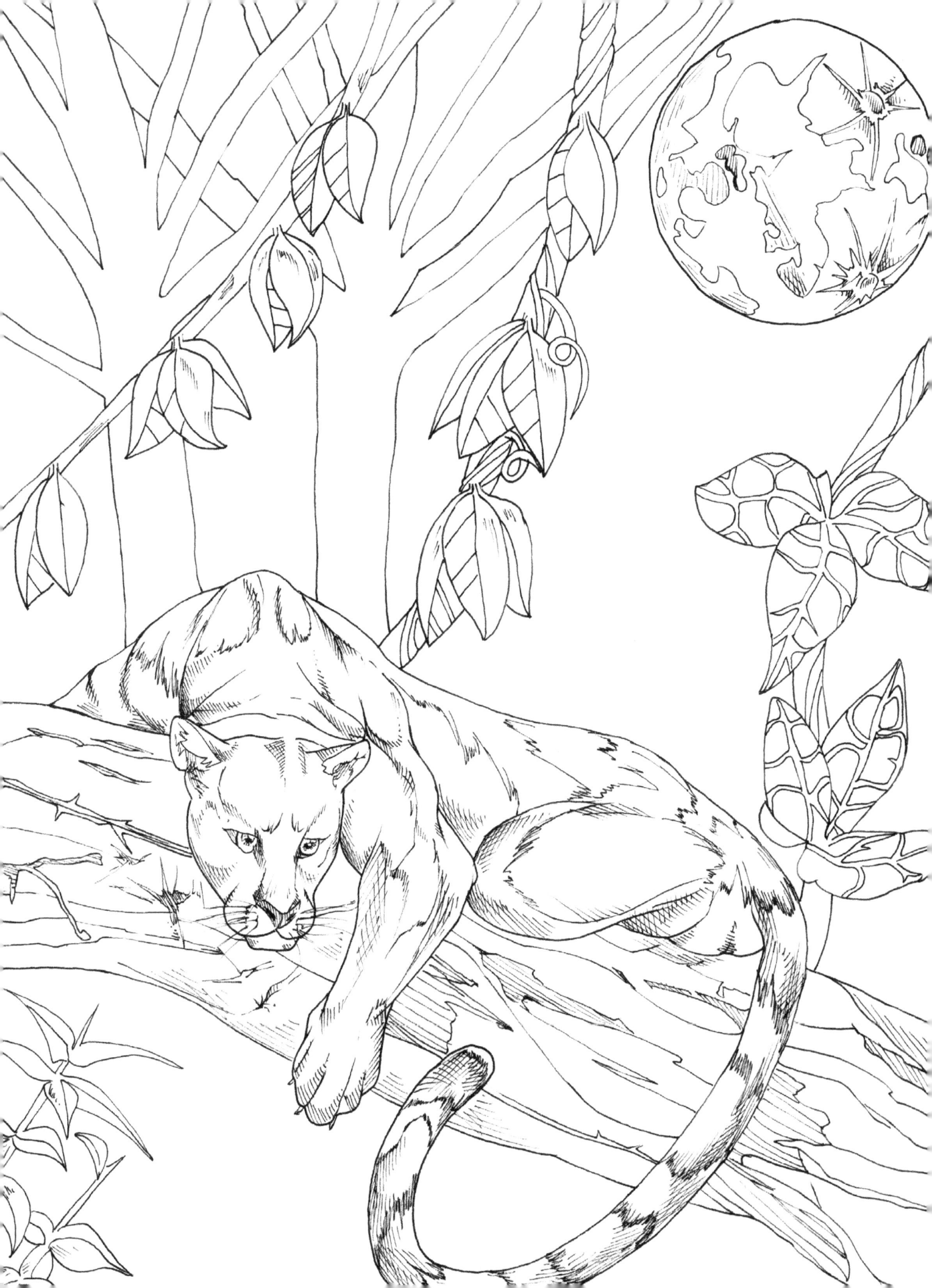

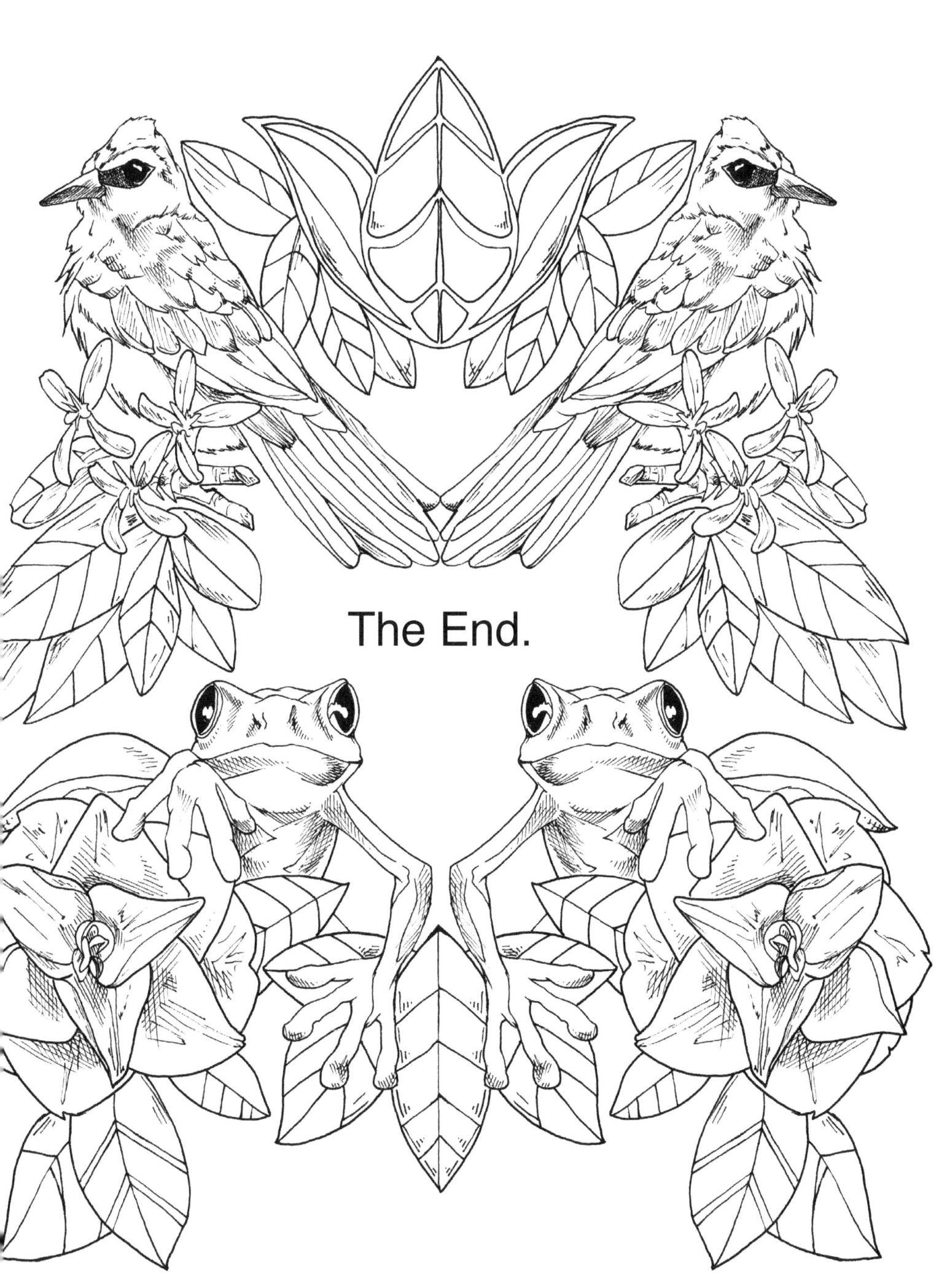

The End.